The *Promise*

MY TIME WITH A WOMAN
AHEAD OF HER TIME

Cynthia Chauvin

New Orleans, USA

Two Dragons International Inc.

New Orleans, Louisiana & Potomac Falls, Virginia

First Edition 2008

ISBN 978-0-9816467-1-8

Printed in the United States of America.

For David

You thought you affected no one.
Your heart and wisdom guided many lives.

The Promise

MY TIME WITH A WOMAN
AHEAD OF HER TIME

Introduction

I had an overweening desire from a very early age I should say I was about 17 to find out the secret of life. What was it all about? I knew there was something there that I should "remember."

I remember meeting a very handsome Englishman I think I was 18. I was invited to a dance, and I thought I would ask him. And he wrote a little note saying if I knew how he danced, I wouldn't ask him, because he danced like a tugboat! So he didn't accept. But he did write in his note, "Funny impression you left with me. Skies in your eyes, but something struggling to get out."

Now I think that sums it up pretty well because there's always been this something that is urging me to realize it, to get it out. As I interpret it today, I would say it has all come out in my writing, which I have been pursuing all my life. My "journal" is a sort of culmination of all my efforts to find out the Truth only to find, through the writing, that it's never "out there." It's always here within. It has been a great search, and it has ended in wonderful flashes of intuitive revelation.

Leonora Nichols

My Mountain

Leonora Nichols lived on Monticello Mountain outside of Charlottesville, Virginia. My first introduction to her was through a mutual friend, Jan Broan. Jan became a client of mine just prior to my moving to Charlottesville. By the time the move was final, we had become good friends. Leonora had contacted Jan for a reference for a credible psychic from whom she could get a personal reading. Jan eagerly passed my name on to Leonora.

When Leonora called me for an appointment, we tried to have a phone consultation at first. After a few minutes, with deep frustration over her failing hearing, despite having a hearing aid, Leonora for the first time made what became an ongoing request: "Cynthia, will you come to see me on my mountain?"

The mere fact that Thomas Jefferson's historic home was a few yards from her driveway didn't concern her. She reigned royally over Monticello. We set a date for me to come to her mountain: Labor Day, 1989.

The day I arrived for our appointment Leonora greeted me at her door. "Are you Cynthia?" she asks, as she surveys me. "Yes, I am," I reply.

There before me stands a small, fragile-framed

woman who is neatly and stylishly dressed. Her piercing eyes are a deep blue almost the color of lapis, with eye whites clear and bright like a summer cloud. Her face has barely a line on it.

"Let's do sit down," she proclaims, as she turns and leads the way. Leonora walks with a cane but carries herself as if the cane is an adornment. "We will sit in my lovely little room," she directs.

She sits down with grace and holds her body in the chair as if she is ready to hold court. I sit directly across from her.

The session begins: "Cynthia, I want to know about my passing. How soon will I die?" her voice rings out without frailty. It is slightly high-pitched and musical. She speaks with perfect diction. I think to myself, That question is no surprise from a 91 year old lady. "Well, Miss Nichols, life is a choice within the environment of experience..."

Leonora interrupts, "Yes, yes, I know all that. But when am I going to die? I have had enough of this body and I don't want to spend another winter here. It is too cold, and I am too isolated."

"OK," I say. "I feel you will be here for part of the winter, leaving before spring." I think for sure there will be some kind of emotion.

"I will order the new blue sweater from the catalogue I saved," she says. She goes on with the conversation as if I have mentioned that her laundry would not be ready on time.

"Now, Cynthia, I am worried about my help. I have two ladies working for me. They are having health problems that keep them from coming regularly. Will I have reliable help?"

I continue the reading: "I see three ladies that will care for you. The two you have coming off and on, and a third always with you."

"But Cynthia," she protests, "I have financial limitations, and I can't possibly afford another person. What will she cost and how will I find her?"

I close my eyes, as I often did in those days, to get a clear picture of the new mystery lady. Much to my surprise I get an extremely clear picture. After a third and fourth time trying to clear away this vision, I relent and tell her whom I saw. "Leonora, I guess the third lady is me."

That's right: the only vision I saw was of me. Me and no pay.

"But I couldn't possibly afford you, Cynthia."

"You don't have to worry. I will come, and there will be no charge."

"Cynthia, you are my angel. God has sent me an angel!"

With her concern about being alone answered, Leonora's voice fills with renewed confidence. "I have written a journal, and I want to know will it be published before I die?"

I am still in shock that I have just committed myself to take care of a perfect stranger. But I continue with the reading. "Yes, I do see it being published, Leonora, but only a small part of it. However, it will be published."

The session ends with me promising Leonora I would come to "her mountain" Monday through Friday, 10 a.m. till 3 p.m., until she dies. I leave mumbling to myself, "Cynthia what have you done? Oh, my God! What have you done?" On the 45-minute drive home I say this over and over. It became a chant.

Now, just like many people, I have made many promises in my life. Some promises, no matter how good the intent when I made them, fell by the wayside. However this promise I made to Leonora is bigger than her. It is my promise to myself to live according to the direction of my psychic ability (higher self), which I believe is my covenant with God. It came down to this: If my mission on Earth is to be a psychic for others, I have to believe in it for my own life and without question follow the unknown.

Finally, as I pull into my garage, I say aloud, "Cynthia if you are going to call yourself psychic, you must live by your own visions."

Cheese Sandwiches

"I remember the cheese sandwiches and absinthe." Leonora is speaking as if she were remembering something that just happened yesterday. "I loved to stop every afternoon at this little café in Rome for my cheese sandwich and absinthe."

Leonora often speaks to me as if I know exactly what she is talking about, and sometimes gets quite agitated when I don't.

"What is absinthe?" I ask with curiosity.

"It was a delicious drink that went well with cheese sandwiches, of course. However, I would only have one or two. It was very addictive," she explains.

"Besides the cheese sandwiches, did you enjoy the rest of your tour in Italy?" I inquire.

"I toured Europe, my angel, not just Italy," Leonora corrects. "I was in my beautiful twenties and had a wonderful time. The art, the music, the freedom, it was so alive, and it brought me to life. I would stay in a city for a month or two depending on how much I enjoyed the city or the lover I had taken. When I became bored with either, I would move on."

Leonora begins her story her face glowing with animation, "After seven years of teaching, I had saved enough money to go and fly away on my own to Europe, and for the first time I left family and friends, and everything familiar. I bought my ticket on the Minnetonka, a wonderful little British ship, and sailed to Paris. I had French friends who left me their little house on a very remote avenue, and there I sat out for a little while, and took French from a professor at the Sorbonne. Then they invited me down to Arcachon, which is way down in the south of France and all that was a great deal of fun.

"But the weather in Paris in winter is formidable. It turns noon into midnight, with fog and damp; and I thought, 'I am going to Florence.' So I went to the American Women's Club and asked whether they knew of a very nice pensione; and they told me, yes, at Bellini's. So I went all by myself I think I was 27 to Florence, not speaking a word of Italian. And it was the most ecstatic moment of my life.

"Florence in 1926 was a little medieval town, unspoiled. I remember writing in my journal, 'I have come home at last. All my dreams are satisfied.' It was really the most beautiful two or three months.

"During that time, of course, I met a most beautiful to me young Italian architect, who was a student in Rome at the Beaux Artes. We had a marvelous time together exploring Florence, and I remember a great deal of uproarious laughter between us for no reason except we were just a happy pagan couple.

"Then, a great and darling old friend of mine wrote

me and said that she was on a world tour and if I met her at the Negresco Hotel in Nice, she would take me to Greece and Egypt. And I said yes. In those days I didn't think anything of hopping on a train and going anywhere. I think back on it now, and I think it is incredible.

"At any rate, I met her at the Negresco, and we went to Greece and Egypt. All this is in my 1926 journal. A couple of years ago I threw everything away, including my journals. But I remember those days so well; I will never forget them. And of course I will never forget my impression of the Parthenon and the Acropolis. I remember writing in my journal, 'I would like to kneel and kiss the pantalic marble of this pure, beautiful, marvelous dream of a building.' The whole Acropolis is out of this world.

"Then we went on to Egypt and Cairo, and the tombs of the kings, and all that marvelous business, which was entirely opposite from Athens, all very earthy and browns. But I was longing to get back to Rome and meet my charming Italian. So the ship went on, and I got my ticket and crossed over to Naples where I had to visit some friends. Then I had a beautiful four weeks in Rome. Finally I had to go home; my money was out. And so I arrived back in America."

Leonora's Journal

Sometime in 1977, Leonora began doing channeled writing in the morning upon arising. Within two or three years she had enough writing to fill two manuscript holders.

The word "Christ," as used in Leonora's journal and quoted throughout this work, describes our connection to God, the energy that runs through all things. It is not a reference to an individual, but to all individuals in their potential to connect to God and become greater than they presently are.

Leonora's journal is written in the language of Leonora, meaning God spoke to Leonora in the manner in which she expected Him Her Them to communicate unlike we humans who, even when speaking the same language, cannot seem to communicate clearly with one another, God doesn't have a problem. God simply speaks in the terminology we expect from God. For Leonora, that was a biblical form. But I urge you not to get lost in the language and miss the message. The content is the pearl, although the context is personal.

I can relate to the idea of God communicating in a biblical manner. Many years ago when I first started doing psychic readings, my language was much the same. I would sit back in my chair, close my eyes, and out would come a voice that spoke in an archaic style. I am sure I must have seemed quaint saying "thee" and "thou." But I'm equally sure the people coming to me found that their message delivered in such a manner was more real for them.

You see I received God's message in a language that I could separate from my "unworthiness." This separation gave me the confidence that the information was coming from a source greater than my lowly self and thus I could deliver wisdom. God, in Her wisdom, communicated to me and through me in words that validated the communication itself. Imagine that!

Leonora was far from perfect and she was not redeemed to "perfection" before she died. It is my belief that our perfection is in knowing our connection to God, not in the perfection of our behavior. We make the Christ-energy live through the acceptance of our imperfections and the imperfections of others, and by bringing this acceptance forward through our thoughts, words, and deeds.

***

Be still, my child, and write. For the time has come for me to speak. But I speak only when man gives fully and absolutely his Being to Me, where I AM. Now be very still and write only what you are hearing inwardly, that the Truth which you seek in your deep heart may be further revealed and more fully experienced.

The human mind with its personality must be very carefully and purposefully disciplined and prepared, that the full glory of the indwelling Christ may shine out. This is the purpose of this effort. This is what you long for and this promise is within your reach, for it is written within your Being. There must be a more consecrated effort, or discipline. The Promise is there, already to shine out in all its glory and effulgence. You have but to keep this goal ever before your inward vision, and hold your attention upon It.

This is the sacred privilege, or gift of God the Father, to man. He awaits deep within the Heart.

This is the Eternal Truth which all must seek and understand in order to grow into the Immortal Being made in His Image.

How else can you receive Him unless you seek Him where He is, and set your heart upon Him where He awaits you?

If your dearest friend on earth awaits you in your home, your house, and you are forever wandering abroad, how can you meet him and glory in his friendship and companionship?

So it is with the indwelling Christ. Think deeply on this.

***

***

At this moment, let thy mind empty itself of all the mechanics of existence and be quiet. So will it be spacious and light that I may speak.

To offer a mind busy and cluttered with things of no spiritual value shuts out the Holy Spirit, which must have the vast open space, and stillness of a living soul, in order to enter.

Space, Light, Peace, Love, these are the attributes that flow in when the human mind is empty of all that denies, of all that obstructs and negates these qualities.

You have but to offer thyself with this understanding as a channel, a vehicle, and immediately the Spirit of Life floods through thy being. He but awaits thy offering, thy love.

As we have said, and we repeat, those beings of Light in the high world are focusing upon those who are open to them for the infinite love and compassion of the living Christ is intensifying at this time, and will pour in wherever there is a human channel.

Therefore, cease not thy effort to give over thy personal self and to listen, listen for the hour draws nigh of the second coming on earth as in heaven.

Amen.

***

Sagatara

"Who is the handsome man in the photo?" I ask Leonora as I point in the general direction of her chest of drawers.

"Which one?" she says coyly, as she raises her eyes and moves them to the place I am pointing. "That was my beloved Sagatara. He was my love." Leonora's story unfolds, "I met him when I was working in an art gallery in Manhattan, and he was up from the little country of El Salvador as cultural attaché in New York. Also, he was an artist and had come up to have an exhibition. So he came into the gallery that I was working in, and oh dear, I have to go back to the vision in England.

"Well, I went to England to live for a year in 1936. While I was there, something triggered a perfectly transcendental and unspeakably beautiful vision when I was in bed one night. I was in the woods, with an unworldly light. It was a sort of twilight, and there were great trees and little violet-colored flowers. And out of the earth came this fountain of living light. Living light! I never saw anything so exquisite. In the vision, I was standing and looking at it, and I kept saying, I had never seen anything so beautiful. The fountain just flowed!

"The fountain of light was a symbol, of course, of life and love, and what we all are: God. Then a veil was drawn, and the fountain disappeared. And then a love was shown to me a human love. But what was I supposed to do about it?

"Well, through much trial and error, the years passed, about ten years, and I never found that love. Finally I thought, 'This is enough. I'm going to absolutely speak the word.' So, motoring to my art gallery that morning, I said: 'Let this love shown to me in vision come forth into this very day. Let it come forth!' It was a deep demand upon the substance of life to bring it forth.

"Then I forgot about it. And I was sitting in the gallery at my desk reading a mystic book, naturally called The Candle of Vision, by George William Russell who wrote under the name "A.E." Then an imposing looking man was standing opposite me looking at a picture. I just saw his back view. I was looking at him and he turned around and looked at me, and there seemed to me to be a strike of lightning, a sort of recognition. He came over and asked, 'What are you reading?' I replied, 'A.E.'s Candle of Vision.' So we talked, and he said he was in New York for his exhibition, and would I come and see his pictures at such-and-such a gallery. And I said, yes, I would. Of course, I was supposed to be tending my business of selling pictures at the gallery, so he departed.

"But before he left, right at the entrance, he stooped over and kissed me on the forehead, and said: 'Who are you? What is your name? Why do I feel as if you belong to me, as if you were myself in a woman's clothes?' Then I remembered, 'speaking the word' that morning. And I replied, 'Well, you will soon know who I am.'

"From then on it was both agony and God knows what it was. Very soon I took him home to my dear, beautiful parents to have dinner, and on the way there I asked, 'When did you lose your wife?' And he said, 'I haven't mentioned a loss.'

"So there we were: He had a wife.

"On the weekends I lived with my parents. I told my father I was staying with a friend in the city during the week. I often wondered if they ever knew I was living with a man.

"It was the most extreme love anyone can imagine. It obviously goes back to another incarnation."

She continues, "Look there on the bookshelf. I have several of his beautiful books."

I go to the books and pull them out slowly. They are very old, and the bindings are beginning to give way. You could tell Leonora has read this man's beautiful words over and over again.

Leonora is perched in her favorite blue chair, which is directly in front of a window. The window shines with a beautiful view of the gardens that circle her cottage. I deliver the books to her as if I where handling precious artifacts.

"Sagatara gave me a manuscript to read in which he was a Spaniard, and he came from Bilbao in northern Spain. He was a Basque with light blue eyes and fair skin.

"The manuscript is this book. The book is Spanish, so possibly you can't read it, and I can't read it. But the manuscript he gave me was in English and it's the most fantastic thing. It's not related to life on this planet at all. And he did the extraordinary illustrations you see in it. He wrote it when he was about 20. They brought it out in a hardcover edition just two or three years before he died in the city of San Salvador.

"Sagatara was evidently a great figure in Latin America because when he died, he had a state funeral in El Salvador. His daughter wrote me and said the flags hung at half-mast all over the country, and the President of Mexico came in a chartered plane all very impressive.

"Sagatara wrote seven books, mostly folk tales of the Indians in El Salvador, and they're all in the University of Virginia Library in the Latin American section. He was also a painter. And he was a tremendous philosopher, a follower of the things that I was interested in. We seemed to have so much in common.

"I feel that he was very much an Atlantean from the lost continent of Atlantis. I read that some of the descendants of Atlantis can be found in Basque Spain. Maybe it's so.

"Here," Leonora says as she opens a book. "Look on the first page, Cynthia. See he has drawn a cartoon of himself. He was a man that had a peculiar affinity for all water, for the ocean; and you can see a seahorse in his ear, and a sort of fish around his eye. He always said that he would not die in his bed. Instead he would walk out in the ocean and go as far as he could, and then go under. That was his plan for himself. But it didn't turn out that way."

In the back of the book that featured the cartoon of Sagatara there are four sheets of loose paper. They are yellow with age and the ink is pale. The handwriting is hard to read. I hand them to Leonora. She reads aloud with just a few glances at the brittle paper.

"Litany and a Soundless Song of Love Blwny

Thou art as the wind
Blowing through my heart,
A wind of love, a wind of beauty,
And my heart a flute.

So intense Thou art
(just by existing)
And so unceasing
In beauty and charm,
That I sing,
And sing,
And sing,
Continually.
Strange forces,
Colossal forces,

Super eolian forces
Blow past my heart of flute.

This melody of Love
In the quiet, starry, night
Of my devotion to thee
This song of Love
That I give to thee;
This song of love
That I have from thee;
This song of love that I am.

Blwny of mine
Incomparable,
Dreamy and ineffable,
Indelible
Imperishable,
Unutterable and
Indefinable;
Flower and leaf;
Pearl and shell;
Harp and sigh of melody;
Path and distance;
Dawn and star and light;
Pain and delight;
Smile and tear;
Mirror of my desire;
Echo of my prayer of love;
Thou exist

The Promise

Beauty in flesh;
Face of silver,
Eyes of sapphire;
Hands that Kiss
When they touch my hands

Thou appearest to me,
In virtue,
As rampant as an archangel
Of God,
Crushing (thy foot of gold)
The head of the dragon
Of New York
(dragon of a thousand tongs)
The husky city of old and now

No woman is like Thee;
O my only!
No woman uses
Thy aura of diamond
(More precious than any treasure)
For thou art Blwny,
Queen of the fairies
Crowned by the Queen of Heaven
With a crown of glittering dew
At the hour of dawn.
Sagatara

Blue Wine

! Oh fountain of down,
Clear Fountain!
Gate of new world rich in love and harmony;
Leonora: through you I come,
Through you,
Thunder of my silence;
Silence of my astonished love
Give me your hand, angel of light;
Press it, so I know you are also a woman.
Press to mine your lips gently,
And let me drink the blue wine of your soul in silence,
Blue wine of the gods!
Silver and sapphire;
Wine of purity;
Aquarian liquor,
Sweet water of Beauty, Goodness and Justice;
My blue water of eternal rapture!
Sagatara"

There is total quiet for several minutes.

I break the silence, "You must have loved him very deeply."

She responds, "Sagatara felt that our love was forever and that he would like us to go through a symbolic marriage service, so he wrote a ceremony for us. There was a church on Fifth Avenue in Manhattan that I particularly loved. Sagatara wrote a beautiful ceremonial marriage service. We went to the baptismal font of this church, and he spoke the words and put this ring on my finger. The ring is a Rosicrucian ring. He had it engraved in Spanish: Sagatara and Blwny: today, tomorrow, and forever. He called me 'Blwny,' which means 'blue wine.'

"Many years later when I moved to my cottage near Charlottesville, I looked for the ring and couldn't find it. And I thought, 'Oh, well, it isn't here. It got lost in my move.' Then one day I saw it in the most conspicuous place, and I knew he had put it there. It was where I couldn't have missed it, in my bedroom. It was right down on the floor by the bed staring at me. I can only think that's so typical of him. I don't know how he did it!

"He loved me more," she says, as she seems to move into the present. "He was convinced I was his true soul mate. I, however, was not as sure. Anyway, it was such a relationship of destiny. For ten years we did the best we could."

"What happened to Sagatara?" I am almost afraid to ask, thinking that some terrible thing must have occurred to take him away.

"He was recalled and so he returned to his wife in his little country of El Salvador."

"What about a divorce? I mean obviously he was deeply in love with you, and you him."

"Sagatara was Catholic and a very well-respected man," she replies. "He could not possibly have divorced his wife. Besides, I did not want to marry him, and it was time to move on to other things."

Leonora's eyes move back to the picture on the dresser, she smiles as if she was questioning the decision Sagatara had made so many years before.

"Sagatara, of course, was the name I called him, not his birth name. His birth name was Salvador Salazur Arrué," she said. "He claimed he became Sagatara when he was with me, and all his beautiful poetry came to him only as Sagatara. I was so young. I met him when I had just turned 50. Yes, 50. And I loved him until I was 60."

I move from my seat, a blue flowered footstool next to her, with the precious cargo in my hands. I enter the first book back to its place. Clearly marked straight lines of dust making the placement of each book to its original spot easy. I noticed tucked inside another well-read volume a slight edge of blue paper.

"Leonora" I ask, "are these more of Sagatara's poems?"

"No, no, no," she rebukes. "Just put them back it is "Nothing, nothing, nothing at all."

"Do you like Chopin, Cynthia?"

"Yes of course," I answer. "Although I am not really sure which one he is," I mumble under my breath.

Leonora walks into the living room looking for her tapes of Chopin.

I return to the book and pull out the blue paper. My eyes reading as quickly as possible the well designed words in blue ink.

A Birthday Poem to Sagatara Oct. 1950

Everywhere
The leaves are falling,
Like tears
Silently, swiftly falling,
Tears the color of wine
Lachrimachrist: wine
Of the "tears of Christ."

So are the years
Falling from me,
Sagatara.
The golden years;
One by one they go

Leaving us like the oak,
Strong,clean,linear
Casting a straight firm shadow,
That no longer wavers,
That no longer fluctuates
With the wind.
You are this oak
Sagatara,
And I the one
Rooted beside you,
And the warmth
Of the October sun
Is mellow upon us,
Even as honey,

And our shadows
Fall decisive and clean
Upon the land,
And they who pass by
Will linger and say,

See, how beautiful are the oaks
Blown free of their leaves.
Of everything that passes
With the wind;
How beautiful they are
Bared down to Truth
Standing side by side
Each casting a shadow
As sharp and clear
As light.

Leonora Nichols

Elegie

Leaf
Falling on yellow leaf,
And the farewell cries
Of little song birds
Lifting
On saddened wings.

Mists

The Promise

Drifting
Lingering
Close to the earth,

Why as we stand
Huddled together
Watching,
Waiting,
Listening,
Nothing is heard
Only the reiterated word
Of leaf
Whispering
To leaf,
And what can be seen
But the veiled
Discarnate
Dream
Of hill
And phantom stream.

Leonora Nichols

***

To be this channel, pure and open and dedicated, is thy morning prayer. So be it.

Thou hast but to listen with thy whole heart this day, and the soundless Voice of Truth already within thee will sing out, will flash out like a Beacon Light, for all has been given and is fully present within the Self. This is the eternal secret to remember. The Divine Consciousness has been fully given to man. He has but to cease denying It by letting a false and artificial identity drown out this Truth, like a great noise, shattering His Divine silence.

As man quiets this great noise, this insistent voice of the bodily self, and deepens the silence within his mind-heart, therein shines the "Pearl of Great Price," and within its luminosity dwells the Self as God created It.

Meditate upon this wondrous Truth this day, for the Divine Consciousness but awaits thy recognition and acceptance that He may speak and show thee all things as they are, on earth as in heaven.

***

***

To awaken to Me is to awaken to Joy and Love and Light and All- Knowing. When you awake from a disturbing dream, there is a sense of relief and gratitude that it was but a dream. So it is when you awaken from the dream of mortality and separation. Peace and rapture flow into the Self, and your soul shouts for joy that it was all but a dream.

Desire with all thine heart this awakening, for I AM here, lifting thy being into the Light that thou mayst awaken to Me thy Self, here and now, this day, this hour.

***

Rachmaninoff

Ring. Ring. Ring.

"Hello? Cynthia, my angel, when you come to see me today, bring two of those lovely little yellow zucchini, and a nice piece of salmon." Before I can say anything, Leonora hangs up the phone. "Click" is all I hear after she places her order.

Usually Leonora gives me a shopping list once or twice a week. On shopping days I arrive a little later than my normal 8:30 or 9:00 in the morning and Leonora is reading or listening to music when I walk in. Every day starts in a unique manner.

"Cynthia, do you see the lovely blue bird sitting by my window?" Leonora asks. "He has been there all morning. I believe he loves my Chopin as much as I do!"

I look out the window to see a blue bird perched as if he is indeed listening to the music.

"I have always loved Chopin," Leonora proclaims.

"However, I was very impressed with a concert I attended by Rachmaninoff," Leonora begins to recount. "My beautiful parents took me; I suppose I was about five or six years old.

"After his most wonderful performance, my family

and I were invited back stage to meet Mr. Rachmaninoff. I can still see him," she says with her eyes closed. "There he stood: Rachmaninoff! He was so brilliant I could scarcely contain myself."

Leonora continues, "I had rehearsed for weeks this moment. I knew exactly what I wanted to say. Admirers surrounded him. My parents and I walked over. After a few polite statements of gratitude for such a wonderful concert, my parents introduced me. Rachmaninoff leaned down and picked up my hand like such," Leonora raises her hand as if the event was happening today, "and he kissed it lightly."

"Before he could say a word I said, 'Mr. Macmaninoff, I love you.' I was so overcome by the moment; I forgot the proper introduction I had planned. I even mispronounced his name. Everyone chuckled, including me.

"I said to Mother, 'I will never wash my hand again!' and I didn't for one week. I walked around holding my hand up like it was floating. My hand felt as if it was radiating energy from his kiss. Radiating the genius that was Rachmaninoff.

"I can still remember every note he played.

"I had such a brilliant childhood."

Leonora turns back to her Chopin with a gleam that you know is for Rachmaninoff.

***

As the day breaks and the light of the sun begins to suffuse thy world once more with its life-giving energy and warmth, so it is with the dawning of the Son of God within thine heart. Let His glory rise and suffuse thy entire being this day. Let Him come alive as thy self. Each breath, each heart-beat, belongs to Him.

This Christ, this Interior Son must rise each day, each hour, even as the physical sun is doing, spreading the life-giving warmth of His Presence throughout thy day.

As the sun mounts the heavens and the mechanics of existence occupy thy thoughts and activities, remind thyself of this dawning, this elixir. To keep it ever present in thine heart is the discipline required of thee.

Remember this at the noon hour; and when day is done, think on these things.

***

***

When you are open and sensitive to the world of Truth only, everything around you will speak to you of the Divine, of Truth. You have but to have ears to hear and eyes to see. These living moments are aflame with Truth. Therefore, let not a second, an hour pass without listening, without seeing, for the Divine is the only reality.

These quiet moments in the first hours of the day belong to the Divine reality of your being. You are listening, you are recording the "still small voice" which is speaking from within your heart.

This is the Truth you are seeking. This is Cosmic-Knowing. This is reaching out and touching the spiritual world within

Your tendency is to belittle this effort, to shrug it off as of no significant importance and to look elsewhere, or to another, for your inspiration. Can you not understand that your own Inner Divine Self can be the only Source of that which you seek. There is no other for you in this respect, no matter how noble or illumined.

Therefore, we caution you to consecrate all your aspirations upon this sacred center within your own individualized Divinity and slight it not, for the outward expression of the remaining years of this present incarnation depends upon this.

***

Finding the Cottage

Leonora is sitting, staring out the window. As I walk in, she looks up to greet me. "Look how beautiful my mountain is today with all its lovely flowers."

We look out the window at the meadow. "Yes, Leonora," I rejoice, "Your mountain is very beautiful. How did you find such a special place?"

"I would come to visit friends here. Edie Nash, the owner of this property and a prominent social leader in Charlottesville, always invited me to stay at her lovely little cottage. This cottage was built for President Franklin Roosevelt. You see? All the doors are big enough for his wheel chair. The furniture in my bedroom was the furniture he used."

She continues, "After Father died, I decided I wanted to live on my beautiful mountain. Edie offered me her little cottage. I don't think she is very happy about making the offer," Leonora says with a gleam in her eyes.

"What do you mean?" I question.

"Well, I think she made the offer because she thought I would be dead in a few years. Instead, I just keep living and living. Oh well, now she just has to wait a little longer to have her wonderful little cottage back."

Leonora moved to her mountain sometime after 1962.

***

There is an alchemy of the spirit that transforms all negative emotions into their opposite. This is not difficult to achieve, but requires only a small leavening of the whole lump of human thinking, by injecting into the stream of consciousness thoughts of power and strength and joy. These qualities are all there within, but need to be activated by use, by love, by faith.

Bring them out into the now this day and you will rise up with the strength of an eagle. Do not wallow in the grasp of self-pity and weakness, but with a steady intent of the spiritual will, lift yourself out of this mortal grip which so quickly holds the human self, as in a vice.

Lift, I say, my child; lift into thy place of Love and Light, and rejoice that thou art this instant free of all weakness and alive to Joy and Laughter and all that belongs to pure spirit.

***

Healing Father

Seated in a chair outside her cottage with a blue scarf and black sunglasses, Leonora looks like a movie star from the 40s. The sun beams around her as I walk up. She is reading.

"Good book?" I inquire.

"I am reading the only book, my angel: The Divine Healing of Mind and Body by Murdo Macdonald-Bayne. Have you read it?"

"No, I am sorry, I haven't had the pleasure," I reply.

"This is the book that saved my father's life." With a little help she walks inside. She points to the many books on the shelf. "You know, I have read many wonderful books, but this book is the treasure."

She sits in her favorite chair with her face still lit by the sun. "I found it many years ago, and I knew instantly it is the way. Then it proved itself," she said.

"You see, my father had become ill and was in the hospital with internal bleeding. The doctors did not know what was causing the bleeding, and he was getting worse every day. I was so worried. I was meditating and praying one morning when I remembered a passage from the book. I knew the words would heal my father, so I began to read aloud passage after passage. I could feel my soul filling with the power of God. I repeated over and over again, 'Father you are healed. Father you are healed.' I did this until I was completely exhausted.

"Then I called and told my father I would pick him up the next morning and bring him home. I told him he was healed, and there was no reason to stay there any longer. The doctors were outraged. My father was still bleeding, and the reason for it still unknown; but I insisted he was healed. I picked my father up from the hospital the next morning. The bleeding had stopped in the night.

"I have no doubt this is the way it is supposed to be," she says.

***

To write as you are doing is a tremendous aid in keeping you in the atmosphere of Truth, of Spirit. Without this effort, as you have realized, the moment-to-moment realization of your Oneness passes without your being aware of it. This Oneness this Attunement or Atonement is the living and vital Fulcrum upon which all rests.

It must become the Way, for it is Life Life Eternal. There is no other Way or Life. Understand this, for this understanding is the Open Door to the Kingdom. To be conscious of this Divine Coincidence of the human with its Divine Counterpart is the immortality that must be accomplished here on earth while in the body of flesh!

Therefore, to record this Truth as it takes place is a great aid in stabilizing this Unity, this Oneness and, we repeat, as it takes place here and now. This is the purpose of the quiet moments in the first hour of the day.

Therefore, let this Truth be the dominant note of thy existence. Let it be sovereign in thy Consciousness throughout this day.

Amen.

***

***

This month is a sacred month within thy calendar. Treasure it as such.

The great inflow of the Christ Light intensifies at this time. Be still and feel it enfold thee and lift thee into its radiation, its afflatus.

Deepen thy silence that He may speak to thee, that He may lift the veils from thine eyes. That He may guide thee into the Centre of all Light and Love and Truth. It is the time for this. For He cometh, He cometh to those who are ready.

Be still, we say, and keep thy heart, thy face turned toward Him and toward no other. Understand what we are saying: no lesser light will bring to you the "Pearl of Great Price" which thou art seeking. There is but One who will show it to thee.

Hearken to His voice only, for the day of Salvation draweth nigh.

***

The Failing Corpse

Leonora is looking in a full-length mirror.

"Cynthia, my angel, why am I stuck in this body? I should be able to just lift myself from it. I am tired. This is not the way it is supposed to be. I am not supposed to be trapped in this failing corpse. Look at it. What a mess."

***

Do not try to plan your unfoldment. Do not be impatient and grab hold of these quiet periods with your human mind. Your task is to be serenely confident of the sovereign power that is guiding you. As we have said, the ego is always at hand to interfere with the Divine, to take the inspired moment and manipulate it to its own size and measure. The voice of the ego is loud and aggressive, while the Divine speaks always with a "still small voice."

Therefore it is necessary to cultivate the quietude, the silence we speak of so often.

Be still, and know. This is the Way.

Over and over we urge you to let it flow. Watch and wait.

Creation of the New ever flows from the unknown moment.

An undisturbed and open heart is the absolute necessity dedicated to the Divine, trusting in the Divine.

This is the Path.

***

***

All thought and especially when it is charged with feeling or emotion makes an indelible impression upon the others surrounding you.

This is thy Book. For each one of you are writing a Book, a Life Story, to be read and judged as you leave your present body and incarnation.

Thus, man faces his own creations, and must judge them himself. There is no other judgment day but this.

It is, therefore, of utmost importance to watch your thought world, that you may review this earthly life without pain or regret. Opportunities lost are as painful for the soul to observe as deeds badly performed.

You are fortunate to have this privilege of silent communication now, for as you absorb and live the Truth that is flowing into your mind, you will bring your Book, your Life Story, to a happy conclusion.

Meditate upon this, for life is a most sacred gift, a treasure, and must be realized as such; and each is held responsible for his use of this gift.

***

I Only Wear Blue

"Come in, Cynthia, come in."

Leonora is sitting on her sofa, opening a box. "I have purchased a sweater, a beautiful, blue sweater."

"It matches your eyes," I comment.

"Of course it does, Cynthia. I don't wear anything that doesn't match my eyes."

I run a quick inventory in my head. Everything I have ever seen Leonora in is blue. I do mean everything. From scarves to pajamas to sweaters, blouses and skirts, all some shade of blue.

"Ever since I was a child I have only worn blue," she says, as she tries on her new blue sweater.

***

To live in the shining moment is the secret. If the heart or mind becomes dull or heavy, a crosscurrent has intervened and the glow, the Truth, the Light of the moment has been overshadowed. Observe this and be on your guard. All should be unshadowed Light. To enter the New is to be free of the past, free of the old self with its egoistic reactions and small, unloving thoughts. You are being tested every moment, every day. Watch, I say, and pray without ceasing, for the time is now for the New Birth, for the Christ Presence to create a New World, a New Earth, a New Consciousness. Be of the New. Be ready, be loving, and let thy Light shine.

There is no other way to dispel the darkness, to bring down my heaven upon earth. Be very quiet, very simple, very peaceful. For those who are Light bearers are preparing the way for the building of the New.

***

***

My child, this pressure you feel within your being is but the ever-present urge toward perfection. It is the Spirit, the Great Spirit, Love itself, calling to you to return. Do not mistake it for human unrest, for as the heart hears and responds, so do you lift to His Presence. Welcome therefore this pressure, this call. As you still the human element, the earth-consciousness opens up to the vast inflow of the Infinite, moment-to-moment. Feel it this moment, and let it be a living continuum of moments, of awareness of His Presence. So will you enlarge your consciousness of Truth, of Life, of Love, and the Peace that passeth understanding will permeate every aspect of thy life.

Look therefore into thyself and see, for the Light therein will show you thyself and all those who are of the Light. For there can be no separation in the Light that is God.

***

Never Gild the Lily

"Cynthia, you have beautiful eyebrows, but you wear too much makeup," Leonora says. "Remember, never gild the lily. When I was a young woman, I only wore a little powder and lipstick. I was quite beautiful and had a very lovely body.

"My beauty served me well."

***

During these quiet Communions when the heart is lifted and vibrates with the higher energies of Truth, these are the moments to cherish in thy life. They will reveal to thee far more than all the gathering of thoughts from other minds.

The Truth that lives within thine own being is the only Truth that thou canst know, that will transform thyself, and so thy world.

Be still and savor deeply what we are saying, for the threads that hold these moments are very tenuous and delicate, and can be easily brushed aside and lost. Therefore, treasure them, my child, as the pearls of great price, for they are the gift of the Eternal.

***

***

Every day brings a new opportunity to grow spiritually, once you dedicate yourself to this goal. That means, of course, absolute attention to the Inner Voice. As you cultivate this Interior attention, you become more and more integrated until at last there will be only one you, and that will be the one invisible to you now.

This is your goal, and it will bring you untold joy not only to you but to the vast Hierarchy of spiritual beings that have followed this path at one time or another, and are watching and waiting for the earth to be redeemed in this fashion.

The present moment, what we call the New Age moment, is offering to mankind this renewed opportunity. And many can partake of this vital moment as you are doing, if they would but listen and then act, taking no thought in the old way. And so today brings this opportunity for you to take another step forward with fresh and unused energy that floods into the consciousness from moment to moment. And we repeat, this energy when used correctly, as we have stated, will open up those windows of the soul out of which you will behold a New world, unknown to your past experience.

So be it.

***

The Borg

As I walk into her cottage, Leonora is half-sitting on her bed speaking to someone on the phone, agitated as always at the difficulty she has hearing.

"Well, Cynthia said I would die before winter is gone. No, no, I believe she is correct, although I do wish it were sooner. No, no. OK, I will."

She hangs the phone up with her usual distain, practically throwing the handset onto the receiver from a slight distance. Just click, no goodbye.

As always, Leonora starts our conversation as if I have been in the room all morning and know precisely what is going on in her mind. Ironically, after a while I do know.

"My older sister, Hildegard, believes you die and go back to the godhead, where you do not know you have existed," she says.

I ascertain the conversation was with her sister.

She continues, "What do you think, Cynthia?"

"Well, I think God went through a lot of trouble to create so many people to return to oneness without any selfhood," I reply. "Who would love the gods if we all disappeared into oneness? I believe we become individual parts of the whole. We become more of who we are, not less."

Leonora looks at me satisfied. "Yes, of course, Cynthia. I believe this also."

"What were you telling her about dying?" I ask.

"My sister was worried I would die just because you told me I would. I told her the message does not create the outcome. I think she just doesn't want to be the last to leave. I am sorry, I refuse to stay any longer just to make her feel better about being alone."

***

Again we say, deepen thy confidence in all that is of the Light the Light that ever flows from the Christ, from the One. Look upon all that confronts thee, that challenges thee, not as evil but as an angel in disguise, strengthening thy faith in the One Truth, the One presence. The greater the challenge, the stronger must be thy faith. There is nothing to fear, as we have said. Strength is what you must build upon. With faith in thy God, and the strength to keep it one-pointed, nothing can touch thee but the Love and Truth, which is even closer than breathing. The Light overcomes and dissolves every shadow no matter how fearful it may appear to be. Rejoice in the glory of the unfolding divinity all around thee. Taste with thy soul the uncontaminated freshness and beauty that is awakening in the nature kingdoms. The young new leaves and blossoms are symbols of the resurrecting principle that stirs the heart and soul to lift up and awake from its dormant state, and realize that this is the Divine ever-calling to all creation.

Drink of this pure water that overflows from its living Source, the great Heart and Soul of all Cosmic life.

Shadows may lurk behind thee, but the Light ever shines upon thee and before thee.

Fear not and press on and never falter, for where there is love in thy heart, nothing can overshadow thee.

***

***

Oh my child, if you could but hold, hold to the moments of ecstasy and wonder that fill thy soul as you watch the great sun rise in a glory of Light; if you could but sustain this rhapsody, thy inner and outer world would become one. As we have said, man and the Universe are partners in this great drama of creation, for one companions the other. Be not blind to this Eternal Truth, for as you open up all avenues of thy self, to this absolute, inescapable Oneness, the interplay can flourish and nothing, nothing will be impossible to you. You, mankind, belong to the Universe, and the Universe belongs to you in all its infinity and glory. How then can there be misery and lack and all the rest that men have created in their refusal, their obstinate refusal to understand this.

Let this vision of Oneness, of Wholeness flood through thy consciousness this day. For each day, each hour, each moment, offers you this Truth that you may partake of the limitless joy and bliss and freedom of Creation as it takes place. You need nothing, nothing else but this realization.

Therefore, do not limit or rob thyself by turning elsewhere.

***

Beautifying

"Cynthia, will you tweeze my eyebrows?" Leonora asks. "I don't know where all the hairs come from. And look I have a hair on my chin. Can you imagine? This is simply not acceptable. I am supposed to sit in my chair and simply lift my consciousness out of my body. The body should not fail. Do you believe we need to deteriorate like this?"

"No," I respond. "I not only believe we should be able to lift our consciousness out of our bodies, I know we should be able to ascend with our bodies like Christ, Buddha, and many other spiritual leaders have already done."

"What do you think about my wave?" she responds. "The hairdresser cut my hair too short. My lovely wave is not correct. Can you fix it?"

The quick shifts in conversations are standard. Leonora will start a subject and suddenly dart from here to there, sometimes returning to the original point and sometimes not.

She watches me in her handheld mirror and instructs me on how her wave should be done. I try but can tell she is less than happy.

She says, "Well, that is better I suppose," then hands

me the mirror and takes the brush.

She brushes and curves her hands around her hair until she gets the wave she wants.

"Now. That is correct."

***

You must have a clear idea, an inner picture of what you are aspiring to achieve. As we have pointed out, Nature is the great mirror before man. Symbolically she holds the secrets of the spiritual universe.

The human soul can be compared with the seed within the earth. This is an obvious and old concept, but nonetheless a descriptive and precise one to aid in spiritual understanding.

It is an age-old question that every man or soul must face sooner or later, and that is the piercing of the darkness into the Light. What you are therefore trying to do now is to draw down this Light from the interior Sun, which will quicken the life within the seed, that it may rise up and the two merge into one Light.

The important thing to hold to in your meditation is the realization that potentially the full flowering is there within yourself; and therefore as this potential or seed-self opens up under the benign light of the Spirit, the miracle of the New Birth takes place.

Each flowering in the nature kingdom is the acting out, again and again, of this Mystery Drama.

The necessity is to know that only the individual self and its dedicated efforts can draw down this Fire, that the sleeping seed consciousness may fructify and unfold in all its supernal beauty and truth.

Nothing in the outer world can do this work. It is entirely an inward process.

The Light of the spiritual Sun, or Son, draws up and penetrates and integrates with the buried, dormant life within the seed-self, or human soul. Thus the great, creative Mystery Drama, which is life on earth, is repeated in the human kingdom, and a new flowering takes place. Meditate upon this theme.

***

***

To foster a dual selfhood is to separate the self from Self, and to block the peace thou art seeking. This blockage is the heavy load mankind has placed upon his own back, a weight that can only be lifted by turning to the Source that knows not this barrier.

Cease then, my child, to foster this false separation of part from other part, of human from its Divine counterpart, for how can wholeness be achieved if you hate the one and love the other? There is but one unifying principle in the universe, or power, and that is Love. See the human, even the human body, through the eyes of Love, and you will become integrated into one Being. There is no other way.

Heed our words and let only the Light of Truth, of Love shine upon thy human selfhood, body and mind, this day, and all will be under the control of the Holy Spirit. And when night comes thou wilt feel a vital New force harmonizing thine entire being, and will sleep with peace within thy soul and within thy body.

***

Grocery List

A message has been left on my answering machine.

"Cynthia, my angel, when you come up my mountain today, would you bring my salmon? I would like four nice pieces, and maybe a little chicken. Can you bake a chicken today?"

Click.

***

When I say, "I am the Light of the world," what does this mean? On the human level it means that the I AM is the Light or life radiating out from the conscious being of the Eternal. And this Light, this I AM, has been given to man to realize in full, for I AM is the everlasting affirmation of life eternal.

This is the Seed within the being of all that is self-conscious. As this Divine potential quickens and unfolds, man's true Selfhood will expand into the fullness of the universal I Amness. "Be still and know that I Am." "That I Am" has no other significance.

Understand this, meditate deeply upon this, and all the activities of thy life will reflect this light, this truth, this life. For I AM GOD, and thou (man) art the Son, and there is nothing else for you to know at this time.

***

***

As you deepen your stillness, your Communion with me, the more creative you will become.

This is the great paradox. To be deeply quiet, consciously quiet, brings you into the Universal Womb of Creation, into the peace that is productive. To let your mind be repeatedly brought back to world thought, with its disquieting images, robs you of the peace that is needed for spiritual progress and understanding.

It would be wise, therefore, during the day's activities to watch your thoughts and to remind yourself frequently of this profound Truth, that your spiritual destiny unfolds from the deep inner calm and serenity of the soul, and never in the flux of the phenomenal world.

***

Milk Toast

Leonora and I are standing in the very small space that is her kitchen, with appliances that date back before I was born and with barely enough room for one, much less two. I am cooking milk toast for Leonora under her strict supervision. She begins telling me about the parties she once had in her little cottage.

"Every year, Cynthia, when my sister came to visit, I would have a great party in her honor. Watch the milk, Cynthia; it must not boil. All the prominent society of Charlottesville would come." She begins listing names that sound like tires, cars, and presidents.

"They all came," she continues. "I would cook my very wonderful salmon mousse. We would have champagne with it. It was a very tiring event. Put a little salt and pepper now on top of the toast, dear. When my sister became too old to come, I stopped the parties and the invitations to other people's parties stopped coming to me. I only have a few visitors now. Now the milk toast is ready. Don't leave the pot on the stove, Cynthia.

"How delightful milk toast is," she concludes.

***

It is a question of freedom from the old. As you, in thought, free yourself from all old patterns of reaction or belief, that which is ever New and unconditioned can come into being. It is so simple; for Divine Truth is always a clear, pellucid stream of Light, unsullied by past usage.

When we say, "Be still," it is in this deep stillness wherein the ever New can flow. It becomes blocked and contaminated only in the separated fragmentation of the ego state.

To heal this splintered self is the purpose of all spiritual disciplines. The joy that cleanses and integrates this self, which has through self-will separated its conscious being from its source, is the joy of recognition, of recollection of its true state.

A breakthrough such as this brings immediate relief from the human bondage and barriers that so tragically obstruct the Divine Light.

Rejoice, therefore, in these moments of illumined contact, wherein the Light of thy True Self can shine.

***

***

When you look out upon all life, all people, through the eyes of love, immediately boundaries go down, resistance dissolves, and harmony flows in. When a question of relationship between persons becomes blocked, know that the wall is but an imaginary one and needs only this realization for it to disappear.

See everyone within thy world through the eyes of love. Feel the flow of love, the joy, the radiance, and let it flood through and out. In this way, there can be no static or blockage within thy thoughts or feelings, nothing to negate or deny the loveliness, the joyous momentum of love.

Go forth, then, knowing that Love is ever before thee lighting the way. How then can you doubt or hesitate to take whatever step the Spirit of Love suggests?

***

Metropolitan Museum

Leonora's living room and dining area are combined into one room. The room is rather large and surrounded by windows and French doors. The entrance I use is an oversized side door leading directly into the middle of the room. As you walk in, you face a fireplace. To the left hangs a huge portrait of guess who Leonora, in a blue dress. Under it was a very cheap plastic blue sofa. Everything in this room, with the exception of the old blue sofa, is priceless.

Leonora is on the phone in front of the fireplace. "It is not correct. My father, Henry Hobart Nichols created the style. You absolutely must get this correct in the catalogue. Yes, thank you."

Click.

"Cynthia you must help me. I have written this down, but I am afraid the Metropolitan Museum will get it wrong because of my handwriting. You see, they have asked me to write about my father's work for their art catalogue coming out at Christmas. It must be made clear; my father's art came first. Many copied my father's technique and became quite famous for it. Now it is time for my father's works to be appreciated as the first in this form. Can you write it, my dear? Make sure you say exactly what I have said."

"Maybe I should take it home and type it," I reply. I look at her for a response.

"That would be fine, but you must do it quickly. I only have a few days to respond to the museum."

***

Inspiration and Vision are a vital part of the New Consciousness, for these qualities flow from the Divine, and they will invite Cosmic Consciousness.

Therefore, hold to the inspired Vision of a New Earth a New Humanity at One with God and all Life, a Humanity attuned to the Universal Brotherhood of all created Beings.

Such a world exists on the Higher Planes, and must be brought forth here by the inspired vision of men that it may be on earth as in Heaven.

Therefore do not hold back from living intuitively this vision now. Let the "still small voice" of thy soul direct thy thoughts, thy activities, that thou mayst be at One with those who are in the vanguard of the New Race.

There is but one Now the living, present moment. Be awake and aware at this point.

This must be your discipline: to let the living waters flow into this Conscious moment-to-moment awareness.

***

***

The cosmic clock regulates the duration of the form, but Eternity is the home of the spiritual Being using the form. That is why we repeat so often the "Eternal Now" for that is where thou art.

Eternity is ever around thee, is everywhere present, for the timeless, spaceless presence of life, of truth, of love and Eternity are one and the same.

I AM the Eternal, and all that I am is Eternal. To practice the presence of God is to live in the Eternal. Man's outer life is conditioned by the clock. But his inner life should flow with the Eternal, unbound by time or space or the inventions of men.

To feel thyself to be Eternal is to experience reality the deathless state. To live in the "Eternal Now" is to enter the stream.

***

Living History

Walking into Leonora's bedroom, you face her bed slightly to the left against the back wall. This single bed is original to the cottage and was used by President Franklin Roosevelt when he was staying there. It is very unusual in that it is a single bed, but with four tall, ornate, carved posts. It isn't until ten years later that I find out it is part of a matching set.

From the bedroom there is a door to a sunroom. FDR's personal aide stayed there. Leonora uses the sunroom as a place to write. It contains a chair with blue floral print cushions that sits next to a small table and a day bed.

Along the wall in her bedroom are bookshelves filled with very old books. A chest of drawers adjacent to the bookshelves displays pictures of Sagatara. A chair, ottoman, table, and lamp are stationed together. This is the chair Leonora sits in to read and to listen to Chopin the chair she thinks she should be able to sit in and lift her Consciousness to God.

Everything in Leonora's cottage is aged. You can feel, see, and smell the long life in all her personal belongings, as well as in all that belongs to the Roosevelt cottage. They are not just antiques.

They are as Leonora is: living history.

***

There is no hiatus, no break in the Eternal as It streams forth, as It flows forth from the Infinite Life, which is God.

It is ever flowing, whether man is conscious of It or not. You have but to be silent and receptive and It is present in all its immediacy and power and wholeness. It is indeed the Fountain of Life. What can be clearer than this symbol, than this Divine message?

As we have said, when the human mind reaches a saturation point and is full to overflowing with the ineffable Truth of Being, Cosmic Awakening will then take place.

This is the purpose before thee. Meditate on this and rejoice that this Truth encircles thee as an armor of light, and be not faint-hearted nor impatient.

***

Lecture for the Inmates

It is Monday morning and Leonora is putting books back on the shelf.

"How was your weekend, Leonora?" I ask.

"I had a lovely visit with my friend, David, and his wife. I always enjoy his company. He has been such a support for my writing. He doesn't do anything to get my journal published, but he does encourage me that it will be. I don't really understand why he believes that. I gave his wife a few of my lovely blue scarves."

Although I do believe Leonora liked David's wife Mary, her focus is definitely on her relationship with David. I don't know exactly how Leonora and David met.

Leonora continues, "David is a teacher at the Staunton Correctional Center. A few years ago, I gave a lecture there on Plotinus. It was marvelous."

"Who was Plotinus?" I ask.

"Don't you know Plotinus, Cynthia?" She looks at me with disbelief as I respond.

"I assume he was a philosopher, like Aristotle or Plato?"

Leonora's response is quick. "Absolutely not. Aristotle, Plato, and Socrates thought the mind was everything, and they were Greek. They were small-minded. Plotinus was the only correct one, and he was Roman, not Greek. He believed we all emanated from God and that our incarnations continued until we reached union with God again. We are only a mind such folly! Can you imagine, Cynthia? Now, where was I?

"My beloved Plotinus, whom I brought myself up on, he is absolutely fabulous, and doesn't get enough attention. He was a Neoplatonic philosopher in the second century A.D., and not a Christian. Nobody seems to know about Plotinus. When I met David, who was a magna cum laude graduate at Harvard in philosophy, I asked him if he knew Plotinus, and he didn't know anything about him. So he said, 'What would you think if I brought you to a group of my philosophy students at the Stauton Correctional Center and you gave a talk on Plotinus?'

"So, David drove us to the prison," she continues. "After passing through several locked gates we arrived at the main building. A lovely, very large, black prisoner at the main prison building greeted me. I could not climb the stairs to the classroom, so he simply whisked me up like a feather and carried me. He was so gentle with me, as if I were porcelain. I felt like air.

"It delighted me to talk about Plotinus because I have loved him ever since I was a girl. He was a great cosmologist, and he said that the Universe is arranged as a general arranges his army, in different ways of being; it has different tasks.

"I ended the lecture with my thoughts on Jesus." She begins reciting the lecture, "I feel that Jesus, the Christ, has been given this planet, and it is his job to evolve consciousness on planet Earth. As this wonderful Aquarian Age begins and we're in it now the Christ as he appeared as Jesus is very near to us, and he speaks wherever there is an open channel. I've had several instances of his appearing.

"So I feel that we all should realize that Jesus, the Christ, is now nearer than ever for our availability in this New Age, which has dawned, and is going to be a spiritual age.

"I have given many lectures on Plotinus, but never was an audience so absorbed. There was total silence from the prisoners as I spoke. I could see their minds filling with knowledge and their hearts opening to receive the greatness of his work. It was a very fulfilling experience.

"I will teach you Cynthia, I will teach you all about Plotinus."

"That would be wonderful." I reply knowing I had very little to say in the matter.

***

To listen to the bodily self is to listen to the voice of the serpent, for its purpose is to tempt you away from your God-self, to lure you away from the Light, thereby strengthening its hold upon you, Heed not this self, either in health or in sickness, for it will bind you with a thousand threads, as a spider binds the frail flying creatures that touch its web.

The biblical allegory of Adam and Eve symbolizes this Truth for with man's fall from Grace, the physical body came into being, bringing with it a sense of guilt, and so a false consciousness, a false identity, from which springs all the evils on earth.

The liberation from this self comes not from physical death but from thy will to disengage, to disorient thyself, thy consciousness, while here in the flesh, from this sphere of influence and enslavement.

All spiritual discipline is to this end. Always remember the soul's felicity lies away from the body and never in or with this self, but in the Christ self-alone, who is thy Redeemer and thy salvation.

***

***

Let us repeat. Each day can be another golden thread in the Tapestry of thy life, if you let His Presence shine into it. From the beginning of these communions, we have warned thee of impatience. Your tendency is to expect immediate results, immediate transformations and manifestations.

As we have reiterated many times, your work is to be deeply still, and to calmly, peacefully, and joyfully know that spiritual growth is taking place, that the Higher Will is fulfilling Itself through you. All must unfold from this still center, gently, naturally, and radiantly.

The design taking shape will then become visible to thy human eyes, thy human understanding. For as these golden threads become stitched into thy life, the whole, one day, will become a creation of Light for all to see.

***

It's Saturday

My phone rings. I lift the receiver to my ear. I do not have time to say anything before Leonora begins to talk.

"Cynthia, my angel, where are you? You are late. When are you coming?"

I reply, "Leonora, I don't come today. It's Saturday."

"Oh."

Click.

***

All will be made clear to you, depending upon your trust, your faith and obedience.

Because of the urgency of the times, the spirit is quickening those centers through which it can speak and work that the New may be safeguarded and established.

The human part of the human being is like a child, and must be disciplined and taken by the hand and led. This is what we are doing. There is, as you know, a vast host or Hierarchy of Beings of Light who are helping in this task. The Christ is the voice speaking through this Hierarchy.

We need only a dedicated heart that has been opened to the spiritual world of Truth.

We repeat, the world of man and the dangerous environment that he has created necessitate accelerating our effort to establish the New energies, lest the planet be plunged into utter darkness. If you read over these notes, you will realize how important it is for you to stay within your center, your self, your sanctuary, and not try to salvage the old. As the plan unfolds, you will rejoice that you have listened and recorded and acted as we direct.

You must absorb and savor deeply all that you have written. A transformation of consciousness is the objective.

Sometimes silence speaks more eloquently than words. Deepen this silence; but let it be as a flame in the "now," and not as a remembering. I speak through the silence as well, for I never forsake thee. I am that Silence as well as the Voice speaking in thy heart.

Rest, I say, for the present in that deep and living Silence. Meditate there, for within this stillness burns the fires of revelation.

***

***

The fact that you feel the deep need, the inner compulsion to continue to turn to these communions each morning is an indication of your spiritual growth. You have free will, and can turn or not turn. This is the point to remember. To choose to turn to the "still small voice" speaking within thy heart, to voluntarily and prayerfully open this door to the Light is the "way to life everlasting." As we have said in these transmissions, this is what is so profoundly needed at this time and the only way of redemption, whether it is of the individual soul, or the life of the planet itself. There is no other way, for the Light can only flow through the open consciousness of man on earth. In this way, he becomes the arbiter of the fate of the world, as well as of himself.

To offer thyself, to see thyself as this channel, this open door is to be a co-worker, a co-creator of the New World.

Go forth, then, into the Light of the New day before thee, rejoicing that thou hast the foresight and perception to understand this.

***

Is There a Hell?

"Cynthia, do you believe we will be punished for what we have done?" Leonora queries.

"No, Leonora, I believe we punish ourselves. When we see the bigger picture, we know everything has a purpose and we stop the punishment."

"I am worried, Cynthia. Worried I may be punished for my father's death."

Even though I have become accustomed to our unusual conversations, this one throws me.

Leonora continues, "My father was ill for many years, and lived with me. We had a housekeeper caring for him, but he relied upon me heavily for his emotional needs.

"I had been caring for father for a long period of time and needed some time away. Friends invited me to visit for a long weekend. I knew father wasn't feeling well, but I did not care. I had to get away or go insane. Father died before my return. If I had known he was going to leave if only I had known. I have been worried God will judge me for allowing my father to die alone."

"Leonora, I know neither God nor your father judges you," I respond.

She looks at me and says, "Good. I am glad that is

settled." "I have never liked sex very much." Leonora continues.

My mouth drops open as we go from her guilt surrounding her father's death to her view on the "useless act of sex," as she puts it.

"I cannot understand why people think it is so wonderful. Sagatara looked as if he were dying. I thought it all a bit amusing. Once he became so overwhelmed, he lay down on me and thrust with such force he lost his balance and his elbow went into my eye. You know my eye has bothered me ever since? Silly man."

Inevitably she asks, "Do you like sex, Cynthia?"

"That depends on the partner, Leonora. But yes, I do love sex." She looks perplexed at my answer.

Many times I have sat in awe of Leonora's life this time she sits in awe of mine.

***

The antidote for evil for all that divides and separates, is Love. When resentment, or hurt pride, or self-righteousness usurps the consciousness, replace these dark emotions with the Christ-Light.

Remember, all negative energies become potent forces and shape themselves within thy environment as power centers. Beware, therefore, of such indulgence.

To build thy thoughts upon a negative emotion is to build a prison-house, for they become as chains about thy soul.

Take heed, my child, and be vigilant, and watch for the signs that change the inner climate of thy mind from Light to dark. All disease, all imbalance, are images of thought that have rooted themselves in the shadows, never in the Light.

***

***

We speak so often of the moment-to-moment awareness. What does it mean to live in the "shining moment"? Let us examine it. Even physically, does not the breath of Life occur only moment-to-moment? You do not live on the breath you breathed yesterday, nor on the one you will breathe tomorrow, but only with the one you are breathing now, at this holy instant. And then another breath comes always in the present moment. Think of this as your life, unstained with guilt or fear, as it flows from the timeless into time.

If you can discipline your conscious mind to understand the full implication of this fact and concentrate your attention upon it as each breath, bringing with it Life, flows forth into the present moment, your mind would be sublimely free from all that the time-ridden ego and the profane world would project upon it.

Do you understand? Your life flows from God, instant-to-instant, ever pure, ever free, ever new, and from no other source. Stop and meditate upon this miracle. Are not the waters of a spring flowing freely from its source identical with that source? You who are Life, who are aware that you are alive, must you not then be identical with your Source, which is God the One and only Life there is? If you can make this leap in consciousness, you will have passed the gate and entered the Eternal.

***

Circle of Light

I pick up the phone.

"Cynthia, you must come up my mountain now. I am dying. I am sure of it."

I try to reassure her: "Leonora, I don't think it's time."

"Yes, I am sure I will die today. Hurry!" Click.

When I arrive, Leonora is perched on her bed speaking to someone on the phone. In spite of the small size of her bed, her little frame seems engulfed by it. "I am leaving today," she said to the person on the phone. "I am sure of it. I can feel myself lifting. Cynthia, my angel, has arrived. I must talk to you later or maybe not.

"Just sit, my angel," Leonora continues. "Just sit a moment. You have been so good to me, Cynthia. What can I do for you?"

I think for a moment, and then say, "When you get to the other side, I would like you to send me help with my work."

I explain my desire to find my own creative power and to pass on the information to other people.

She listens, but with not much patience, sure that if I take too long she will lift from her body before I have finished. "I will, Cynthia. But how will I remember?"

"I know Leonora," I respond. "We will make a circle of Light that can't be broken by time or space. It will be a circle of the soul." Leonora looks excited and very much alive as we begin.

We join hands and declare to the universe our intent to make a circle of Light that cannot be broken, a bond of our souls. Leonora vows she will help me, and I in turn will help others. We declare, vow, and then declare some more. We sit together with our eyes closed, then open, then closed again. After a very long time we both begin to fidget. The passion begins to wane from our vowing. We look at each other as if to say, "OK, what's next?"

I think Leonora expected she would lift after the circle had been made. Half-agitated, half-relieved, she says, "Cynthia, I don't think I will leave today. What a pity."

We begin our visit over again.

***

When we say there is only God and His Son, it is the absolute Truth that ultimately must be attained by man if he is to fulfill his Divine purpose, or destiny. The goal is set, as we have said. But the journey can be straight and narrow as a razor's edge, or interminably long and devious. It is within man's free will which road he chooses.

The forces of evil seem to be the dominant forces today. They are, as we have said, the dark forces that belong to a false master, and must be understood as such and faced and denied. These forces flourish in chaos, for they belong to the "wilderness" experience of life on earth. They are everywhere at this juncture, and seek to gain control of the earth and men's souls. This is the important thing to remember. "Get ye behind me Satan" is the keynote that will disintegrate these shadows, which come from the netherworld of the Anti-Christ.

It is a testing time for those whose goal is the Christ Consciousness and, therefore, it is necessary to undergird thyself with the Light continually and hear only One Voice. The Drama of Man takes place within the individual self. Here is where the forces conflict and must be met. The choice is always here, where the Light and dark meet.

As the days come and go at this great testing time, you will have, again and again, to make your choice. It is therefore of paramount importance that you understand this, lest you lose this vital opportunity and moment on earth.

***

***

The advantage of writing, as you are doing, is that it makes possible the necessary discipline. There is less interference, both mental and physical, as you write in this fashion. The concentration that is needed has been achieved, enabling you to listen and hear the Voice within. Thus, communication becomes possible.

Everything rests upon this listening and stillness. Deep meditation is another matter, and a withdrawn, cloistered life is not a necessity at this time. For the objective is to gather together those souls who are capable of Communion in one form or another, that we may be able to use those who shall be the Forerunners or nucleus of the New Humanity.

Always remember that this moment on earth is the apogee of an age, an age that has peaked to its limit in defiance of the Law, and therefore must destroy itself, that the waters of Life may rise again, purified, as a New Wave, a New Earth, a New Race.

Understand this, for the disappearance of the old will inevitably take place.

It is of great importance therefore that this is understood, lest the souls we have need of be overcome with panic, and thereby be lost in the breaking up of the old.

***

She Is the Devil

Carrying a small bag of the usual supplies, I walk into Leonora's home unannounced, as I always do. Leonora has a visitor, a woman in her 50s with long, gray-black hair, wearing several amulets around her neck. Leonora introduces us. I politely chat for a moment. Leonora seems unusually standoffish, but I pay little attention and move to the kitchen to prepare the small hen I have brought.

In short order, Leonora becomes more interested in how I intend to cook the hen than in the conversation she is having with her guest. She comes into the kitchen and inquires, "What spices will you be using on the hen?" She then begins soliciting her guest for suggestions on how to cook the bird. There we are, the three of us looking at one small chicken. A great discussion on its preparation ensues.

After a few minutes, Leonora sees her guest to the door and returns to the kitchen. I am placing the bird in the oven. We have a little more conversation about the temperature at which we should cook the hen, and then we move to the blue sofa.

"You enjoyed your visit?" I ask.

Leonora replies with a question. "What did you

think of her?"

Being from the South, and always too polite for my own good, I search my mind for a way to say she gives me the creeps. "She is unusual. Why do you ask?"

I can see the familiar sparkle in her eyes as she responds, "She claims to be my friend and a psychic."

"That's interesting," I say, but not really thinking so.

"Yes," Leonora rejoins, "She says I need to be careful of you. She says you are the devil."

I have to admit I am now interested.

"Are you the devil, Cynthia?"

I start to laugh, and blurt out, "I have an ex-husband that would agree with her. What do you think, Leonora?"

"I think you are my angel and I told her so."

***

There is Evolution and Involution, a winding up and an unwinding. The form unfolds through the laws of involution, and Self-Consciousness unfolds through the process of evolution.

Evolution draws out, and involution closes in. Men become egocentric through the process of the one, and Christo-centric through the process of the other.

The earth Consciousness has reached its nadir of materialization and must shift its center of gravity and return to its spiritual center, that Consciousness may be evolved to the Christ level.

This is the Divine purpose of the New Epoch on earth to quicken the potential of all those who are ready to move forward to this point of gravity. For the Christ is calling forth His own, and the souls of men must hear and make ready to return.

It would be wise to reread and meditate deeply upon all that has been given thee in these few communications.

Even as water reaches a boiling point, so too does meditation reach a saturation point, and Revelation then takes place.

But without the necessary fire beneath the water, it will not boil. So it is with the Fire of Truth: unless it is held steady and constant within the mind, the barriers that enclose the Self will not dissolve and the Truth be released.

Therefore, keep thy lamp lit, that the shadows enclose thee not. There are many windows of the Soul, but only One Door that opens to where He stands and awaits thee.

Meditate on this in thy deep Heart.

Amen.

***

***

You will discover, more and more, the universality of Truth as it flows through different and on the human level, separated human channels, unknown to each other.

This is filling you with wonder as you recognize the release of the same Truths, expressed sometimes even in the same words and clothed in the same thoughts, but coming from other selves and other places. This is to be expected, for what is taking place now is a leavening and preparation for the New evolutionary forces to bring in the higher energies that will expand the human consciousness. The present initiation, or preparation, is bringing to those who are ready and open a New urge, a New impetus, a New desire to be a part of this channeling of the Light which is pressing everywhere for release. This Light, which is growing in momentum, will gradually encircle the earth as more and more open to it, and thus the New Epoch will be grounded and so will the planet evolve and unfold into a Higher Consciousness.

This is what is being asked of you and all those who are lovers of Truth, and who understand that God and His Son are the only Creative Source in the Universe.

And who is God's Son but the spirit of Truth and Love ever-flowing from the Father into the soul of man as the Christos.

***

Lawrenceville

The painting of Leonora hung over the plastic blue sofa is grand. I believe it is the only painting Leonora has kept of her father's work, and the only portrait he painted. Her father, Hobart Nichols; her mother, Wilhelmina Von Stosch Nichols; her grandfather, Henry Hobart Nichols, Sr.; her uncle, Spencer Baird Nichols and God only knows who else were all artists.

Growing up, Leonora lived with her family in the Lawrence Park Community in Bronxville, New York. Lawrenceville, as it was known, was a planned community of artists exclusive to those who were successful in their art both nationally and internationally.

"Cynthia," Leonora says, "only the best, only the geniuses, were invited to live there. You had to be invited. I grew up in an environment of grace and beauty. The most talented painters, sculptors, writers, and potters of the time surrounded me. There where schools for any art you desired to study. There were socials and garden parties. So much beauty " Her voice and her mind fade into fond memories.

"I came from a rather distinguished family of artists," she continues. "My parents were both painters, and my family was all professional people, and wonderful people. They were all Washingtonians. Father, being a painter, wanted to get his reputation in New York. So he moved us and built a beautiful, old studio house in a little, unspoiled village outside of New York Lawrence Park West, and there I grew up from the age of about 10. And it was a beautiful youth with wonderful parents and wonderful grandparents, and a wonderful garden and wonderful friends, and I was very blessed all the way through."

It was clear that Leonora was immensely proud of her mother and father and of their status in the global art community.

"In my endeavors to find my own artistic voice, I was nourished by all," she continued. "My family and the extended art community family were all there, leading, guiding, teaching. I investigated everything from pottery, to stained glass, to work with inlaid designs on precious metal."

She hands me a small silver box with an inlaid blue bird on its top. "This is one of my pieces," she says. "I used my little silver box to hold my face powder."

I open the box, and a small amount of the face powder falls out. I ask, "Why did you not pursue your art?"

"Cynthia, my darling, I just never produced anything to my satisfaction."

Always the consummate perfectionist, Leonora never found her voice in art.

Later she gives me the little silver box with the

very blue inlaid bird, still containing the remnants of her face powder.

***

Because of the manifold diseases and miseries within the framework of human existence, there is always lurking within the conscious and unconscious mind of man a fear of the material body and what it can inflict upon the self.

This is the great darkness that has overshadowed the human race since the Adamic myth of man's fall from Grace, and it must be destroyed. This false image of a material self is helpless in the face of disease and all the evils lodged within the race-mind of historic man, and it is this fear that the body will reflect in one form or another. As you consciously or unconsciously absorb into your mind the picture of human beings sinking down into disease and death, so do you fear this fate for yourself. It is a natural reaction. But be not afraid, for this Godless image of life on earth must and will be reversed, and the true fact of life replaces it. The fact is that man, as God created him, cannot suffer either disease or death, and this Truth must be brought back into its rightful and sovereign place in the consciousness of all mankind.

Until this is established as an absolute, you (humanity) will continue to fear the physical body which holds within its ancient memory the seeds of old age, disease, and death, and all the disasters created by the ignorant bodily or human mind.

Understand this and replace fear, this false image,

with the eternal Truth that, from instant to instant, there is only One Law in operation, God's Law of rhythmic harmony. And there is in the entire Universe, no one and nothing that can overthrow this law.

Once this is understood, and when it is understood and accepted by all mankind, there will remain neither fear nor its dark manifestations within all the Kingdoms of the earth.

***

***

As we have said, you must love impersonally. Your consciousness must know one supreme attachment and that is to God, to Christ, to the Universal Good. This is important to remember at this time, for all depends upon it.

It was said some two thousand years ago, "Love the Lord thy God with all thy heart, soul and mind. This is the first Commandment." When the individual self has given itself to this supreme Love, all else unfolds. It is so simple to understand, for it is God who, in His incomparable love, responds and gives.

When the individual soul looks only upon the Divine Beloved, the human entity is blessed without measure.

My child, this is thy lesson for today.

***

Findhorn, Scotland

Always in the middle of a conversation Leonora veers off out of the blue onto another subject.

"Do you believe in fairies, Cynthia?"

"Fairies?" I inquire.

"Fairies," she replies.

Without waiting, she carries on. "I did so want to see the fairies at Findhorn. They were there, and many people saw them, but I did not catch a glimpse of one."

Not wanting to be left out of the conversation altogether, I jump in with, "Yes, I believe in fairies."

"That's good," she replies. "The Conference for World Peace was held there and I attended in deep hopes of seeing the fairies. I saw no fairies.

"Do you know about Findhorn?" she asks of me. And without time to answer she begins, "Well, Findhorn is a very amazing spiritual community in a remote part of northern Scotland. Peter and Eileen Caddy founded it. Peter was out of work, and he had only a small unemployment check. And he had a little mobile trailer they call them "caravans" there in a group of caravans on sort of a dump heap on sand dunes, right on the North Sea.

"I had read a book about Findhorn, which is a remarkable story. There were only three of them at first.

One, Dorothy McLean, was in touch with the Elemental Kingdom, and got her messages straight from what she thought were the Elementals. I suppose you would call them 'fairies.'

"Then Peter and Eileen Caddy came, and through following the directions of Eileen's channeled writings, and Dorothy's intuitive psychic touch with the Elemental people, they built on a massive sand dune, in some miraculous way, a beautiful Edenic garden, with fruit trees and flowers of every sort. I was dying to see it because I have always believed in fairies my whole life. I adored fairies, and devoured fairy books, and Arthur Rackham's marvelous pictures of fairies. I still do.

"So in 1976 I went, and I lived in one of their caravans with an English girl. I wasn't very young then. I was 79. The talks we attended were very interesting. There was a seven-hour seminar on the wholeness of life. But the speaker that I found the most fascinating and had an immediate response to was Sir George Trevelyan, the great British leader of the New Age. He carried me away with his eloquence and his love of poetry. He always brings poetry in everything he writes; he was brought up on poetry.

"I do believe he was my soul mate."

For a brief moment she pauses in thought.

I speak up, "Really?"

"When I met him he embraced me in his long form," Leonora continues. "I felt as I had before in my dream of the fountain. I remember that dream with such clarity. I was walking in the forest when I came upon an open field. In it was a fountain, a fountain of mystical light silently flowing. I stood without movement in its ecstasy. I called out to God. The fountain disappeared, and in its place was God's energy. His arms folded around me, whispering my name. I was at one within His energy. I have never felt the magnificence of the dream on earth until I met this man. I wonder why we met when I was so old, and he so married. It was a relationship not meant for this lifetime," she says with a note of sorrow. "I am thankful though that I met him.

"I believe I have the poem I wrote about my vision in the little blue book next to Kahlil Gibran," Leonora points. "Would you get it for me dear."

I hand her the book. She reads aloud with strength.

"Within Is the Fountain

From where I stood
In the strange wood
I saw It.

Gazing in wonder
As the waters rose and fell,

A Fountain of Light
Emblazoning
The wood.

This was no earthly
Familiar thing.
These living waters
Flowered forth
Into the dusk,
And fell again
More softly,
More silently
Than falling light.
I stood transfixed
In ecstasy,
Breaking the solitude
With a cry!

O Loveliness
O God
O Radiance
Unutterable.

Even as I marveled
The veil was drawn again.
The rapturous waters
Uplifted before mine eyes
Flowed forth no longer.

The twilit wood
The pale flowers
All had vanished.

Only love stood there,
And he folded his arms
About me,
Calling my name
In dear familiarity
Over and over."

"Isn't it a beautiful vision?" Leonora blue eyes filed with energy.

"I would say it is the only vision any of us need." I reply.

"At the conference, Sir George read my journal and insisted on writing the Forward," Leonora speaks with pride in her voice.

"I have a copy. You know Cynthia he is a very important man and it is a great honor to my long years of work for him to write such a beautiful piece.

"Here it is my angel would you like to read aloud." Leonora says this more as a command than a question.

I begin the first line.

"Never mind I will read."

With great jubilation she reads.

"By Sir George Trevelyan.

"There is a real place for books, which have the authentic ring of the Christ Source speaking within. For many people, they are invaluable for reading in bed before we put out the light and turn to sleep, for the entry into sleep if lifted mood is of paramount importance. I think of volumes I have love and treasured: God Calling and Christ In You by Two Listeners (anonymous), God Spoke to Me by Eileen Caddy, The Quiet Mind by Grace Cooke. Here is another of great beauty, coming clearly from the same high source. The title expresses the great Truth: Within Is The Fountain.

"I recommend it to you not only as an excellent-bedside book, but because it points the way for which we all must strive. A spiritual awakening is taking place on a wide front. It manifests in an infinite diversity of expression, as if a flood of New Consciousness and spiritual energy is beginning to flow. Many have gone questing for guru and much study is given to the spiritual teachers. But in the last years many have learned that ultimately the only real teacher is within us.

As Browning wrote:

Truth is within ourselves. It takes no rise
From outward things whate'er you may believe.
There is an inner centre in us all
Where Truth abides in fullness, but around
Wall upon wall the gross flesh hems it in,
That perfect clear perception, which is Truth.

"We live in dramatic days when change is foreseen on all levels. Everything points to the likelihood of a great transformation of consciousness in Western man before the end of the century. This may be accompanied by outward changes, which must be accepted and welcomed as a cleansing of the polluted planet. But for each one of us the challenge and responsibility is to take control of ourselves the one part of the universe we really possess and can change.

"Thus in these years there is nothing more important than finding the Inner Teacher. Truly this is the way to God, for the I AM is the Voice of God. All outward study and questing leads to the same goal the Divine within each of us. Here is the ending of the GrailQuest, so relevant to our time.

"This little book is a beautiful example of thegoal achieved. It has the authentic ring of the Divine Voice speaking within. Not only is it inspiring reading, full of wisdom, but it encourages us to feel that we too may achieve this power of inner listening, so that in time the Voice may begin to speak to us and direct our lives. The authoress, Leonora Nichols, lives in Virginia. She is a beloved friend of many concerned with the present quickening of the spirit. Yet this writing is beyond personality, and the name is therefore hardly relevant. The Journal, received and written down over two years, is full of treasures of wisdom and joy. The Christ speaks in this way within us and our lives are changed.

"May this Journal encourage many to work towards their own conscious contact with the Source within. There is a shift now from the earlier trance mediumship to an inner clairaudience, a listening to the Voice. We need not greatly fear deceiving ourselves. Even if at first we are really talking to ourselves and writing down the results, it can be valuable as an exercise. But it is a common experience that when the "Voice within really speaks, there is no doubt of its reality. More and more people will find the Christ flow within in the coming years. We are all on a spiritual journey, and Leonora's contribution by publishing her inspired writings will certainly be an encouragement to many to work for their own contact.

"I most heartily recommend Within Is the Fountain to all who are involved in the movement for spiritual-awakening, which may ultimately be the salvation of mankind.

She finishes.

"Well that's that lets see about lunch." Leonora moves from the moment quickly as if it was to fragile to stay.

***

As you write, as you listen and record, creation is taking place. What is creation but Revelation Truth revealed. The calyx opens and the flower is revealed. The heart center opens, and from within that sacred sanctuary the Truth flows out.

Let it flow, my child, and be still, and the Truth that is speaking will build its own edifice, its own form, that will harbor the shape of things to come. To be a channel for that Truth, that expression, is thy privilege now.

So be it.

Watch, we say, and Pray, for the time is ripe and the harvest will be garnered for those who await the Bridegroom, and for those who are prepared and ready.

Amen.

***

***

Hold to the love and wonder that stills thy heart when it listens to the Voice speaking within it.

It is easy to push this "still small voice" aside and listen instead to the voice of the world. The world self is an entity, an amalgam of forces built not upon truth, and therefore to survive it must repudiate truth. Its cry is "Crucify, crucify" for it knows that Truth will destroy its sovereignty. And so it will.

Heed not this voice. It will obstruct the Divine purpose unfolding within these communions. It is the voice of doubt and unbelief and ever mocks the purity and innocence of the unworldly. We caution you constantly, for the danger is always at hand, like a dark shadow.

The Truth leads always towards the Light, for Truth and Light are one.

Amen.

***

My Little Blue Car

Parked in front of Leonora's cottage is a small, blue car. I assumed the car belonged to an employee of the estate. After a few months, it dawns on me it never moved from its spot.

"Whose car?" I inquire.

Leonora goes to the window and sees my car and the blue Chevy.

"I haven't a clue," she answers. "Isn't it your car?"

Confused, I looked out the window. "No, it's not mine. My car is parked behind it."

"Oh," she smiles. "You are speaking about the little blue car. It's mine," she says in a matter-of-fact tone.

Blue of course. How could I not know?

"I stopped driving, you know," Leonora says.

"I assumed you had," I reply.

"Yes, it became too much trouble for me to drive to New York to visit my friends," she continues. "The trip was very tiring."

"That is a long trip. Eight or more hours," I say, with a vision of Leonora driving her little blue car hundreds of miles in one stretch.

"When was your last drive to New York?" I expect it to have been some years ago.

"About two years ago I stopped driving that far. And a little later, I stopped driving at all," she says, with a hint of sadness. "Now I keep it for the help."

***

You are listening to me now as never before. My Voice, which is speaking directly to you, can now be heard all over the world through different channels.

Salvation is now at hand through Me, thy Christ. Listen then, Child of God, as never before, and keep thy face turned toward me, that revelation can take place. For only through revelation will the old and dying world be wiped out from thy Consciousness, and the world that God creates be seen.

"I Am the Way and the Truth and the Life." The Way to the New Birth, to the Resurrection and Atonement of all.

Release everything into My hands, for this is the hour when the Bridegroom enters the Bridal Chamber and claims His Own.

***

***

Let thy tears flow. They come from the deep heart. They are the tears of release and, in Truth, of joy. For deeply thou knowest that thou art beloved by Him, and it is this that is overflowing in thy heart. Weep, my child, as the Light floods in and out. It is, as we have said, the waters of thy Fountain, washing clean thy self-hood that thou mayst stand stripped of all that is of the shadow world, before thy God.

Doubt not, for all those who love the Light are being gathered together to save and redeem. Thus the mighty work of Redemption is taking place and will go forward as each one of you understand and offer yourselves for this Divine operation.

Believe in the Invisible Power that is quickening and leavening the human soul, that it may be the open channel that is needed. As we have said, those few who are awake to the Light are being garnered, and will be the Torch Bearers of the New Humanity.

Go forward, my child. Thou art surrounded by Light and are being watched over.

Be at peace. All is well with thee. All is well.

***

It's Not Saturday

Ring. Ring. Ring.

"Hel...," I begin to say.

Leonora interrupts before I can finish: "Cynthia, my angel. Today is not Saturday. What time will you be here? I need you, my angel."

"I will be there about 10:30," I reply.

"Very good, Cynthia. I am tired of zucchini. I want something different."

Click.

Shopping for Leonora was never easy when I brought her precisely what she asked for she would inevitably ask if the store had something else to offer. This day I decided I would bring one of everything she had ever requested.

Walking in with many bags I am greeted with, "What in the world is all that." I hear her but I do not see her.

"Well I thought I would get you a large variety." I respond without visual contact.

"Very well I suppose that is fine. Hurry and put them away."

While my head is in the refrigerator making room for her bounty I try to explain to Leonora I will not be staying this day.

"Leonora," I say shyly, "I have to leave as soon as I put the groceries away. I have a hair appointment at noon."

"I am sorry Cynthia what did you say my angel."

A little less shy this time I recant, "I will not be able to stay today I have to leave as soon as I have put away the groceries away."

I hear nothing from her.

I turn she is directly behind me.

"Cynthia the most marvelous thing, I have prepared a lecture on Plotinus. We shall study him today."

"But Leonora," I mutter.

Before I could offer another word Leonora smiles and says coyly, "Sorry my angel my hearing aids are not working properly so I have taken them out. Now come let's begin my beautiful lecture."

Hair appointment now by the way side, I follow Leonora to her bedroom where she takes her royal position on her blue chair. Before I sit down she begins the lecture.

"Now Cynthia, Plotinus' philosophy is considered very difficult to present because of the tremendously rich canvas he sketches of reality. I think very likely he's been neglected because of this and also because his system is rather elaborate, as is his way of presenting his thoughts to students in conferences," as they were called.

"He's very verbose. He was a man who was so full

of the Divine, and so full of ideas, that it just flooded his consciousness. And he wrote without rereading what he wrote, and without correcting it. His biographer, Porphyry, said that Plotinus didn't care about spelling or punctuation, and it was very difficult to organize his conferences from that point of view. Plotinus was only interested in the ideas that flooded his mind.

"I've written some notes, and I'm going to try to stick to them, because one can get a sort of philosopher's indigestion if we just ramble on.

"Are you comfortable Cynthia. This is a rather lengthy lecture but well worth your stickiest attention." I feel as if she is warning me that I will be quizzed at a later date.

"I am very comfortable." Those were the last words I spoke for over 3 hours.

"Plotinus' philosophy is so rich, and has such profound depth to it, that we must try to be organized.

"We know very little about Plotinus' parents or his birth. He was a native of Egypt, which was then part of the Roman Empire, and he was possibly of Roman descent. He grew up in Alexandria, Egypt. Alexandria was at the time, the greatest center of Greek culture in the world. Plotinus lived from 205 270 A.D. dying at 65 years of age, after spending the last 26 years of his life in Rome. Thus he lived largely in Alexandria and Rome during the early Christian era.

"But, Plotinus was not in any way influenced by or attracted to Christianity. His Divine authority was the

Greek philosopher, Plato, who lived from 427 to 347 B.C. As Porphyry tells us, Plotinus was caught up in the passion of philosophy when he was 28 years old, and he studied philosophy from a great teacher named Ammonius Saccas.

"Alexandria at that time was a very cultured city-where religious and philosophical debate flourished; and there was a great deal of Christian teaching. The Gnostics were there, and such early Christian mystics as Origen, and Clement of Alexandria; these were contemporaries of Plotinus. Plotinus disapproved of the Gnostics. He thought Gnosticism was too honeycombed with Orientalism.

"What is interesting is that although Plotinus wasn't attracted to Christianity, Christianity incorporated Plotinus and the Neoplatonists almost entire. Such great Christian early church fathers as Saint Augustine absolutely absorbed Plotinus. Augustine read Plotinus in a Latin translation. Augustine lived about a century after Plotinus, and you will find in Augustine's autobiographical Confessions quotations from Plotinus verbatim.

"Platonism, which flourished in Alexandria, petered out after Plotinus' death, having lasted several centuries. During Plotinus' lifetime, Plato's philosophy was considered a veritable religion insofar as it tried to channel a rapport between the Divine and man. But after the fifth century A.D., Platonism was completely absorbed into the mystic Christian church.

"There is a great ecclesiastical scholar in England, William Inge I don't know whether he's died yet who was the Dean of Saint Paul's Cathedral; and he loved Plotinus and wrote two very big volumes on him, which I read as a young woman. I have always felt that Plotinus is a man of today as well as of sixteen hundred years ago. To me, the philosophy of Plotinus augments Christianity. It goes into more detail, and it doesn't in any way refute Christian theology; on the contrary.

"So Dean Inge says this of Plotinus: "No other guide even approaches Plotinus in power and insight and profound spiritual penetration. I have steeped myself in his writings, and I have tried not only to understand them as one might understand any other intellectual system, but also to take them as a guide to right living and right thinking. We can only understand him by following him. I have lived with him for nearly thirty years, and I have not sought him in vain, in prosperity or adversity."

"My deep feelings about Plotinus go back about forty-three years. This volume of Plotinus' thought, as you can see, is practically in pieces. (Holds up book.) I wish I knew somewhere I could have it rebound. It was bought in 1946 just 43 years ago.

"I have loved Plotinus with all my heart because I think of him as a spiritual authority on all aspects of life on earth. Although he is sometimes difficult, I have found him deeply poetic and dynamic.

"I'm fortunate in having this volume of Plotinus because Stephen McKenna, who is an Irish scholar as well as a Greek scholar, translated Plotinus in the only English version. And in this book, Miss Grace Trimble has culled from Stephen McKenna's translation the essence of Plotinus. It's really for students like you and me.

"Now as to Plotinus' background and as I say, very little is known we are fortunate in having a short biography of Plotinus written by his great disciple and follower and friend, Porphyry of Tyre. I'll read you just a little from this biography, because I think it's always impressive to get things as direct as they were given out.

"Porphyry's biography of Plotinus was written in 303 A.D., a long while ago; and yet as you read it, it could have been written yesterday. Porphyry says that Plotinus was caught up into this passion to study philosophy at the age of twenty-eight, as I mentioned, and that he found his perfect teacher in Ammonius.

"Like Plato, Plotinus isn't concerned with man's estate in the world. Of course, Plato's great tome, The Republic, tries to apply Divine Truths to government, and so forth. But Plotinus is concerned really with the Soul. Don't be frightened. Plotinus is supposed to be one of the most difficult philosophers to understand. But I find him very clear, and very poignantly beautiful, and a great influence for moral good in the world.

"So, Porphyry says in his remarkable little biography of Plotinus, 'In the tenth year of Galianus' reign, I, Porphyry, arrived in Greece. Plotinus was about fifty-nine when I first met him, and I was 30. I passed six years in close relations with Plotinus. Many questions were thrashed out in the conferences of those six years, and 24 more treatises were composed. Five more Plotinus wrote, and sent them to me while I was living in Sicily; and shortly before his death I received four more."

"Let me explain that the Enneads of Plotinus consist of groups of nine conferences, all with their specific subjects six groups of nine, making 54 in total. Plotinus' class consisted of seminars, and his method was the dialectic process of discursive debate questions. and answers. So the Enneads consist of the conferences of Plotinus, given out in 270 A.D., in the early Christian era.

"Porphyry continues, "Plotinus had a large following. He lived at once within himself, and for others. From his interior attention, he never relaxed, unless in sleep and even that he kept Light by constantly concentrating upon the thought within. Not a few men and women of his position, on the approach of death, had left their boys and girls with all their property to his care, as to a guardian holy and Divine. His house, therefore, was filled with boys and girls.

"He was gentle, and always at the call of those having the slightest acquaintance with him. After spending 26 whole years in Rome, acting as arbiter in many differences, he had never made an enemy of any citizen. At the conferences, he was competent in exposition and he showed the most remarkable power of invention and comprehension.

"When he was speaking, the Light of his intellect visibly illumined his face. Always a winning presence, he then appeared with still greater beauty. Slight moisture gathered on his forehead, and he radiated benignity. Good and kindly and singularly gentle and engaging, we ever found him to be sleeplessly alert, ever striving for the Divine."

"Now this, you must understand, was a philosopher whose one absorbing objective was the Divine. So it's very different from parapsychology and other things of today. This is a mystic philosopher. And his one objective was to experience the ineffable act of absolute union with God. He had no other objective, so everything was relative to that."

"Porphyry concludes:" "For the one end of his life was to approach and become one with God over all; and four times during the period I passed with him, he achieved this by the ineffable act itself."

"I consider Plotinus one of the few holy men that have lived on earth. He is a Divine authority as far as I'm concerned. And there certainly are very few of them today.

"So we have tractates (or treatises, or conferences), each on a different topic, and they cover just about everything. I thought that the best way of presenting to you is to give you Plotinus in his own words. So I'll read a few of the tractates. But in the meantime, I want to outline to you his system.

"Plotinus' system was not unlike Christianity's theology. His whole teaching rests upon the one Divine Truth, the supreme God. He refers to Him as "the Father," or "the Fairest," or the "All-transcendent." And he says, 'God is unity,' roughly suggested. But He is unknowable, being the one God, and unknowable from the point of view of our knowing anything.

"From this One emanates the second principle or hypothesis or person of God. You can look at it as the Holy Trinity in Christianity. There isn't a Son; there isn't a Christ in Plotinus' teaching. And there isn't a Satan. But the second principle he calls 'Divine Minds.' And this is an emanation of the One that is he Intellectual world, the Universal Intelligence. It holds within it all the thoughts and ideas that flow out from the One. And the Divine Mind, according to Plotinus, can be thought of as a sort of mediator like Christ between the Soul and the phenomenal universe, and God the One. In that way, He is a sort of a Son; he can be considered as a mediator because Divine Mind, according to Plotinus, can be known.

"Now the third aspect of this one Divinity is the Soul, and the Soul of the all the All-Soul. That means that this is the formative principle. It looks to Divine Mind and receives all the ideas and all the thoughts emanating from the One, and creates the phenomenal universe, the cosmos. And all Souls your Soul and my Soul emanate from this one Soul. As Plotinus stresses, every individual Soul at its source is this one Soul, or this aspect of God, and every individual has this Light within him.

"On this tractate on the "Complement" of body and Soul I will touch a little bit more. But that is the system. Those are the graded triad as Plotinus teaches it: the Holy Trinity in Christianity, and the one Divine Mind, and the Soul. Those are the three aspects the intellectual world, the creative world, and the one Source of it all.

"Now, I have always found it very confusing to know how on earth we got into this state. What relation has the body to the Soul? And what relation has the Soul to the body? And what relation has the Soul to the universal Soul, et cetera? And he takes that all up in a very interesting way.

"Plotinus calls body and Soul the "Complement." He speaks of it as the "animate," and the animate is the Being part of ourselves. Being, as he says, suggests that which is durable, that which is everlasting, that which is always present. We, each of us, are in Truth Being. This is our spiritual nature. And the body is something else again.

"So the 'Complement' is body and Soul. And Plotinus explains that the Soul is not "in" the body that only one aspect of the Soul, the lower part of the Soul, contacts the body, is attached to the body as an agent to its instrument. And, therefore, he says that the whole thing is to realize this fact, and try to disentangle ourselves from our body as much as possible because the body takes over, as we all know. There's certainly no mystery there.

"So, the Soul is always shining upon the body; and the body appears to be alive because of the presence of Soul, the power and the Light of Soul. Otherwise nothing would be alive. So Soul is life, intelligence, creation, and it is present everywhere. But again, it's interesting to me that Soul is "not in" the body. The infinite is not in the finite anymore than the light of the sun coalesces with the things that it shines upon, and this is very clear. The light of the sun never coalesces with the air; it stays always separate. So Soul is never stuck in matter.

"This is to me a very important point. Because instudying Theosophy years ago, it taught that the infinite sleeps in the mineral kingdom, dreams in the plant kingdom, and awakes in the animal kingdom. I never liked that. The thought of the infinite sleeping in the mineral kingdom is to me very unsettling. So Plotinus makes a great point that this can never be that the Soul, like the light of the sun, never coalesces with matter.

"Now Plotinus says, "Because of the Soul's presence, we feel that the body is alive. But if the body is really a part of us, we are not wholly immortal. If it was an instrument of ours, a thing put at our service for a certain time, then the sovereign principle, the authentic man, will be an agent to this instrument as form to this matter. Thus the Soul is the man. Soul is an essence. It does not come into being by finding a seat in body. It exists before it becomes the Soul of some particular living being."

"Plotinus explains that in the Soul's attachment to the body, the Soul loses its primal sovereign power by this admixture, which we all are only too familiar with. And I think this is so beautifully put. He says, "'All dalliance with what wears the mask of the authentic, all attraction toward mere semblance, tells of a mind misled by the stellar forces pulling toward unreality."

"Plotinus further explains that everything here in this material aspect of our lives is as "a shadow." I mean it's pulling us toward unreality all the time. And it is the purpose of philosophy to direct the Soul back to its original state. That's the whole purpose of philosophy, as I understand it.

"So, Plotinus says, "Our task, then, is to work for liberation from this fear, severing ourselves from all that is gathered about us and striving not to be the composite being, a body and Soul in which the body element is really the master." And this is what he says is so important: that you realize this, for otherwise you go bereaved of that higher Soul, and you are bound then by fate and you are sunken, as it were, in this sidereal system and dragged along with it. In other words, if you don't deliberately understand these things and strive for the higher, then evolution will be your road and that is a very long road. That's the sidereal system; it will drag you along, and so forth.

"Now, again, I have touched upon the fact that the infinite can't be in the finite. Plotinus said, "This can never be. This principle itself is not lodged in anything. All things participate in it; for it is one, undistributed and unbroken entire, yet stands remote from nothing that exists. Unity remains then poised in wisdom within itself. It could not enter into any other. These others look to it, and in their longing for it they find it where it is again.

"So great is Unity in its power and beauty, that it remains the allurer, with all things of the universe depending on it, and rejoicing to hold their trace of it. And through that trace they find their good.

"The Fatherland is there, whence we have come, and there is the Father. You must waken in yourself that other power of vision, the birthright of all."

"On beauty, Plotinus says, "There are earlier and loftier duties than we have here. In the sense-bound life, we are not grounded to know them, but the Soul sees and proclaims them: the face of justice, and of moral wisdom, beautiful beyond the beauty of the evening and the dawn. Such vision is for those Souls who see with the Soul's sight. And all will fall upon them, for now they are moving in the realm of Truth." So you see it's very lofty, and sooner or later we all have to come to it, no question.

"What does Plotinus say of evil? He says that evil does not really exist. He states, "If evil exists at all, it must be situated in the realm of non-being. By this non-being we are not to understand that something simply does not exist, but only that it is something of an utterly different order from authentic Being."

"Plotinus places the cause of all evil on matter, for it corrupts and destroys, he says, "encroaching upon the Soul's territory by substituting its own opposite character." Now we have only to look out upon our world today to see how true that is. The material world, the material sense of being, has substituted its own opposite character to reality as it comes from the Divine. And this is the great challenge.

"So, Plotinus says, "Vice is due to the commerce of the Soul with the outer world, for man includes an inner rabble, which we all know. Man includes pleasures, desires, fears, anger, hatred, lust all these things; and these become masters when man gives them play." But Plotinus always reminds us that to govern these passions is quite possible, because virtue has been given to us by the Soul. And virtue is in the midst of us all the time.

"Evil is here," he says, "where life is in copy." So we live in a very unreal world. We live in a world that isn't receiving from the Source the uncontaminated Truth, pure Truth. We live "in copy." We are doing it now listening to Plotinus, instead of doing what Plotinus did. We live in a receptive world, and Plotinus is the great guide trying to show us his way. And it requires a lifetime of making yourself transparent."

" Excuse me. I wanted to ask you: what he's saying is that man is good unless he is given materials to mix with his knowledge, his Soul? Unless he has something to manipulate?" My first question.

"That's right. He says that man is basically good, because God has given among all this rabble within him, virtue. And virtue absolutely cannot be conquered. In the end it has to prevail. But man must understand that he has this rabble within him. And when hatred overtakes him, or viciousness or jealousy, he has to understand that this does not come from the Divine. It comes from the material sense of life, from the bodily self, and man has to discipline himself, and listen. So the Divine is always around him.

"Now I'm going to read just the last bit of this tractate on the subject of the One. I think we've touched upon Soul that all Souls are one at the base. Again, the tractates and treatises and conferences are all in question-and-answer format. Here is the question: "Are we distinct of this authentic Being as itself present? Or is it omnipresent in the sense only that powers from it enter everywhere?" And Plotinus answers, "This principle is never less than integrally present. All is offered though the recipient is able to take only so much. It belongs to the seeker only while seeking, and to no other." Now that's an important thought that God belongs to the one who seeks Him, and to no other.

"In the same way," Plotinus continues, "soul concurs with the body which it has illumined through and through. That which cannot be diminished will not be absent at any point, because Being is omnipresent but to the realm of Being." You won't find Being in any other realm but the realm of Being, because Being is God, and He never leaves His own garden.

"So now let's just discuss a little bit to end this thought on the One. As I say, I have always worried about the infinite being in the finite; and Plotinus explains that this can never be. We also know there is no Christ or Jesus in the philosophy of Plotinus. He does say that when you experience reality, "He" is gentle and tender, and we have "Him" with us when we will. And that sort of suggests the Christ presence, doesn't it?

"Now, Plotinus said, "Although the presence of God is omnipresent, yet only the competent possess themselves of that presence. The transparent object and the opaque answer vary differently to the Light." That puts the whole thing in a nutshell. Are we going to be transparent, or are we going to be opaque? And it goes without saying that as Plotinus made himself transparent, he actually experienced what very few people on earth have experienced, and that is absolute oneness with God.

"So, the next question is: "What then is the Spirit, guiding the present life, and determining the future?" And Plotinus answers, "It is the Spirit of here, right now; here and now." And the question, "And the God?" Answer: "God, here and now, Spirit God who conducts every life, where even here and now it is the dominant of our nature. This Light shining within the Soul enlightens us, and works it into a likeness of itself."

"This is very interesting to me: we are self-enlightened because we have the Light of God within us, and it's through identity with the spiritual aspect of ourselves that this enlightenment can take place. It works us into a likeness of itself. Plotinus says, "It is therefore by identification that we see the good, and touch it by being one with what is spiritual within ourselves. For the Divine is part of us, and from this we are ever rising. The Supreme is everywhere; He is everywhere in entirety.

"The Soul by nature loves God, and longs to be at one with Him, as the noble love of a daughter for a noble father. The coming to human birth, enlured by the courtships of this sphere, she takes up with another love, a mortal, leaves the Father, and falls. One day, coming to hate her shame, she puts off evil once more, and seeks her Father and finds peace." And we have the story of the Prodigal Son, as the Christ gave it.

"The passage I'm going to end this little talk with is the most famous passage of Plotnius and it's repeated almost verbatim in Saint Augustine's Confessions. What are you to do to prepare yourself to receive the Divine? Plotinus says: "So let the Soul that is not unworthy of the vision contemplate the Great Soul, freed from deceit and every witchery, and collected into calm; calm to be the body, the tumult of the flesh. All that is about it, calm. Calm be the earth, the sea, the air, and let heaven itself be filled. Then let it feel how into that silent heaven the Great Soul bloweth in."

"That is a very beautiful and very famous bit of

Plotinus' teaching. And I will end it on that. I just want to reiterate that Plotinus, above all, from start to finish, is a mystic philosopher. He was a "philosopher" for anyone who is interested in things of the world, et cetera. But he's a mystic philosopher, and his way is "the alone to be alone." His way is the ascent direct ascent to the Supreme. And his way is closing the eyes of the senses, and opening the eyes of the Soul.

So that is Plotinus. I feel that anyone who reads and studies Plotinus is a tremendous influence for moral good. Whether he's the President of the United States, or an Emperor in Rome at the time of Plotinus, I should think that the influence would be tremendous, and we would have a very different world."

My turn "Leonora if you were to try to sum up what has been particularly meaningful to you in your study of Plotinus, what would you say has been of special influence on your personal life?"

Leonora, "Well, I would say that one of the most important things is to know that I'm not stuck in the body in any manner. My sovereign being is my spiritual Soul, and it is using an instrument, and should be absolutely the power. That has helped me a great deal.

"And also that the knowledge that God in His entirety is everywhere present, and there is no place where He is not. God is integrally present and it is up to us to make ourselves, as Plotinus said, "transparent" enough for us to reflect that.

"Plotinus has been a great help to me particularly

concerning the body and Soul, because often one feels victim of this shut-in condition we have on earth. It seems as if an iron curtain falls, and we don't know how we got so bound by matter. And all the mysteries are unsolved. So, with a great Wayshower like Plotinus, it is absolutely an incredible help, because you can look upon everything he says as spiritual facts that absolutely can be verified by anyone who wishes to take the trouble to follow the way, to follow their Being.

"Also, I love Plotinus' emphasis on beauty, and symmetry and balance and reverence for life. these things are very real to me. And in this world today they are all defiled. Symmetry, balance, harmony, and beauty these are all aspects of what Plotinus would call the Soul. You might ask: What is the Soul? What does it look like? Well, this is the Soul. She points to surroundings.

"Beauty means everything to me. I was fortunate to be born with artistic parents; and all these pictures you see here on my walls are by my father and mother. My whole life has been surrounded by beauty. I am very fortunate in that way. It means absolutely everything to me."

I pose another question " You speak about Plotinus' desire, above all, to be one with God. Is that because you have this intense desire, too?

"I have always had that desire. I can't say that I have fit myself for the ineffable act. But it has always, since I was a very young girl, been my desire. When I was 19, I began to read Plotinus and become a Theosophist, and a Buddhist. You name it, and I've looked into it. The Truth has always been my pursuit, because I think it's the most important thing, and it's the only reason we're here.

"There is absolutely no other reason to be here than the pursuit of God and to lift yourself as much as you can out of the material, bodily self. To experiment, and explore that part of yourself which is the intangible part, the invisible part which is the real part.

"I always feel that my love of nature is of great help to me, because I look out upon the beautiful earth, and the universe, and I feel that this is, you might say, "the face of God."

"My love of nature might be one point where my disposition is a little different than that of Plotinus?

"Plotinus says "everything there is also here." He has a very interesting explanation of the universe. If you compare the universe to the body, the upper part of the body is the noble part, the middle part is less noble, and the lower part the least noble.

"And so it is with the universe. Two-thirds of the universe is the noble part. It is full of angels and arch-angels and noble beings and Gods and godly men, and so forth. And the middle part is man; man is between the ape and the angels. And like the body, the middle part of the universe is less than the upper part.

"Also, he says that the universe, Providence, hasar-ranged things as a generalissimo arranges an army. Everything is organized with a hierarchy, with certain responsibilities. So we have in the universe this great hierarchy of Being the Gods, the archangels, the angels, and so on. This is our universe. And we live in a living universe. We have to remind ourselves that when we tune into the good, we are tuning into a living universe, because it is good.

"Wasn't this a lovely afternoon, Cynthia."

"The best Leonora, the best afternoon."

I totally forgot about my hair appointment.

***

Love is the transforming power. This simple and axiomatic Truth is all one needs to understand at this time, for it is the central force inherent in life. If it is reversed, and that reversal brings forth both pain and disharmony, by that very reversal the way will point back to the harmony of Love and that which has been projected by the denial, the reversal of Love, will destroy itself. This is the Law.

When one is heavy with self, and with the barriers and problems that self has produced, one has but to find one's way back to this fundamental Truth, and to realize that love is always at hand as both Presence and Power. And that it is as concrete and as demonstrable as the presence and power of the sun.

Even as the light and warmth of the sun is the agent for all the flowering in the nature kingdoms, so too does selfless love within the heart bring forth all the flowering within the human kingdom.

Let it shine forth this day, my child, and both the visible and invisible world will be aware of its presence, for such is its all-embracing power.

***

Tea With Kahlil Gibran

As a rule, Leonora is reading Murdo Macdonald-Bayne's book on healing when I arrive at her cottage. But on a few occasions, I have found her browsing through The Prophet by Kahlil Gibran. When I am returning The Prophet to the bookshelf, I notice that Gibran had dedicated this copy of the book to Leonora on the inside cover. When she sees me reading the dedication she anticipates my question.

"When I returned from Europe I got a job in an art gallery. It was during that time that I met Khalil Gibran, Sarojini Naidu, and Claude and Said Hussein, who edited a beautiful magazine on Asia. They were a group of perfectly beautiful souls. And then there was a woman who had a gathering of such people on Friday evenings; how I got into it, I don't remember. But I used to go and I was very much younger than all these illustrious people.

"I don't know whether you have read The Prophet by Khalil Gibran." More of a statement than a question, she never waits for an answer.

"But Gibran was a perfectly delightful man. He didn't look at all like the pictures of the Prophet that he drew in the book. He was Lebanese, of course. And

I had the most wonderful time when he invited me to his studio on Tenth Street in Greenwich Village in New York. He read from a manuscript to me, and it seemed to be his book, Jesus, the Son of Man, which is equally as beautiful as The Prophet.

"Look there on the shelf," she points, Jesus, the Son of Man." I retrieve the book and hand it to her. "He autographed it one night at his studio and drew the hand for me it was sort of an insignia of creation.

"He was an intense man," she explains. "I very much enjoyed his company.

"I remember one Friday evening when a woman read from The Prophet. Very statuesque I think she taught elocution because she read so beautifully. Khalil Gibran and this beautiful, marvelous Indian poetess and stateswoman, Sarojini Naidu, were sitting on a sofa in oriental fashion with their legs crossed. As this woman read from The Prophet, I was fascinated to see how they were both weeping. Tears were just pouring down their faces. Khalil was listening to his own writing, but they were overcome with the beauty of it.

"At that evening meeting was Claude Bragdon, who became a great friend of mine. He wrote books on yoga and all sorts of metaphysical subjects and was an eminent architect. Also there was a very handsome man from India, Said Hussein, who edited a beautiful magazine called Asia, and he and I became very romantic friends.

"I remember another evening with Sarojini Naidu.

She wanted to go to Harlem. So Said Hussein and I and Sarojini all had dinner in Harlem. That was a peculiar thing; but anyway, that is the kind of thing we did on the spur of the moment.

"Those were beautiful years when I came back from Italy and worked in the art gallery."

As I watch Leonora's face drift into the present I find myself in envy of her rich life, that is until I think about her comments on sex.

***

There is only one Peace upon which all Heaven rests, and that is the peace of God. As you bring your conscious being to this center, this still point, you will have left the world with all its anxieties, and will have entered an ego less state, a timeless state that is a heavenly state.

The more you practice this discipline, the greater will be your peace of mind and your usefulness on earth as a Son of God.

Pure, conscious Being in all its immaculate innocence, wherein there is no limit to love and its absolute power, will then take the place of the bodily self.

"Be still and know that I am God," has no other meaning than this.

Truth is so simple; there is no need to struggle to reach It, for there is no distance to traverse and no need at all for "the dark night of the soul," with all the agony of self hatred and self guilt that but weighs the soul down and anchors it in the bodily self.

Your goal is to turn your attention, your allegiance, away from this self and enter the great Light, which will consume the past, leaving only the golden nugget of thy Divinity. So be it.

This is the Christ Message at this Christmas Season.

***

***

There will always be mystery, for God can never be fathomed. But, as we have said, the being-part of the human complex is the Divine Potential, or the Word, which holds the Divine Image. Being is the soul, and is enmeshed in the Infinite Light of God.

As the Creatures of the sea live and move and have their being within the mighty waters surrounding them, so does the human Soul live and move and have her being within the Infinitude of God's Light or Life, and therefore this Light is the home of the soul. She draws her substance and sustenance from It.

The purpose of life on earth and beyond is to understand this, and thereby to focus this awareness and extend it into the vast and fathomless Creativity called "God."

This is the sacred gift to man, that he can release evermore Light, or Truth, from within his marvelous Oneness with the Source of all Light.

It is of immediate importance that this evolutionary step be taken, if humanity is to evolve into the Immortal Selfhood it is created to be.

Understand this, and never cease to listen to this Interior Voice, even though the night falls and darkness will seem to invade thyself and thy world. Never fear, for the Light of Truth, of Love, is the one Reality, and will never, never forsake thee.

The Father loveth the Son, and His everlasting arms are about him always.

The Great Disappointment

Thursday, October 12, 1989.

"It has arrived." Leonora starts the conversation before I have fully put the phone to my ear, her voice almost breathless. "My book, Cynthia. It has arrived! I am almost afraid to open it."

"Wait until I get there," I say. "I will bring champagne. Today is my birthday. We will toast the birth of your journal and my birthday. What a celebration we will have. I will be there shortly." Click. This time it was I who hung up without saying goodbye.

I stopped just long enough to pick up a bottle of champagne and hurried up the mountain. My excitement to open the package grew with every mile.

When I arrived, Leonora was sitting in her living room with the package open, raging at its contents. "This is not a book," she exclaims. "This is a pamphlet! Everything in it is wrong. What a terrible thing. I can't believe it. This is not a fountain on the cover. And look at the back cover filled with mistakes. I won't have it. They must all be destroyed!"

Her voice filled with contempt, she says, "It is not bound. It is stapled. How could he do this?"

Leonora was devastated and heartbroken by the

small book that had arrived.

After she calms down somewhat, we look at the publication together. None of my suggestions are comprehensible to her. I say, "Do not destroy the books. Give them to the prison, Yes, the book is thin and has errors. But the message is worthy of being heard."

My voice does not even penetrate Leonora's consciousness. She points out every discrepancy in the book. After taking a long breath, she says, "I will have them all burned."

Her mind is made up. She won't consider any alternative. "I will not disgrace myself and my family by having my name on such unprofessional work."

A few minutes later she calls the publisher and insists that the "pamphlets" be destroyed. The publisher, it seems to me, is a man in Florida whose company took a very small section of Leonora's journal and printed it as an inspirational soft-cover item out of the goodness of his heart. I remember Leonora telling me earlier about his desire to help her see her dream of publication be realized before she died.

Little did the man know Leonora. Nothing short of a perfectly edited, bound hardcover book, with a professionally artistic fountain on the cover would have begun to meet Leonora's criteria.

When her phone conversation with the publisher is over she turns to me and says, "Why, Cynthia? Why would this happen?"

"What comes to me, Leonora, is that the book is

too small. You must publish the journal as it was transcribed "by you."

She replies, "The journal is too redundant. I selected only the best passages about 80 pages."

"Leonora," I rejoin, "it is not up to you to edit what God gave you. He didn't say to share 80 pages. Remember, you told me it said, 'Share these words.' Where are the other entries?"

She moves to her bedroom and returns carrying a pile of loose papers. "Here they are," she says, handing me the pile. Some sheets are handwritten, some typed and, altogether, a mess.

As I take the stack of loose sheets, I say, "The book needs to be as it was given to you. It doesn't matter if it is redundant. The redundancy has a purpose."

"Cynthia, take the journal," she says. "Take all of it. I want nothing more to do with it. I am too old. I cannot possibly put it together. And I will not pay to have it published. It is yours do with it as you will."

I walk out with the papers piled high in my arms. Over the next several weeks, I carefully reconstruct the journal, often with only the color of the ink to guide me. It is a tedious process, but I am determined to return the journal to Leonora intact and in perfect order. When I finish working with the journal, I eagerly go to see Leonora, expecting to bring great joy to her with the completed job.

"Leonora, I have finished your journal. It's back together in its original form," I tell her as I hand it to her.

"That's very wonderful, Cynthia. But I don't know why you went through all that trouble. I told you I don't want anymore to do with it. Now, did you remember my little chicken?" The day carries on as usual.

When I leave that evening, Leonora hands the journal back to me. "I told you, Cynthia, it is yours now. Do with it what you will."

I take it home that evening and we never discuss it again the fulfillment of her lifelong search for Truth, of her long life's journey!

***

All Beauty dwells in quietude, in stillness. In this stillness, the delicate voices are heard. The soft note of a bird, of a woodland stream, and above all, the wordless voice of Love within the heart. This is the silence that is necessary for all communion, whether it be with thy earthly lover, or thy Divine one, or with the great Mother that is Nature.

Solitude, quietude, are lovely words and are the speech of the soul. To listen to this Voice in the pure light that surrounds thee is thy privilege. For it is in this effulgence that thy soul is opening up. It is the Divine Lotus within the heart.

Feel it embrace thee this day, and rejoice that it is so.

***

***

Whence cometh love and beauty into the world, or song or laughter, or longing for the Divine Beloved.

Whence cometh compassion and courage, and the inspired Will to seek thy God.

To meditate upon these things is to reach out and touch Reality is to savor the Essence within thy soul. The calyx separates and opens, and silently, softly, the flower unfolds.

Whose Hand is gently opening the petals, whose eyes are watching and adoring. Who brought thee forth to ponder these things, to see and wonder and reflect the Truth as a prism reflects the light.

The calyx opens and the flower unfolds. Meditate upon this image. Its message, its Truth will open thy heart, even as the calyx opens, releasing its essence into the world of men.

***

The Poor Stockbroker

"Cynthia, would you write a check to reimburse you for my groceries?" Leonora asks.

"Sure. Where is your checkbook?"

"There on the table," she points.

I open the checkbook to fill in the stub. When I am finished she asks me to subtract the outstanding checks and quote her the new balance.

Looking over my shoulder as I calculate, she says, "That is another one who will be glad when I am gone."

I look up at her and she smiles.

"My stockbroker many years ago lost all my money. He felt so badly that he promised me he would send me $2,000 a month for life. I was in my 70s. Look how long that has been now. Well, he shouldn't have lost my money to begin with."

***

In thy stillness, when it is a deep inward quietude waiting upon thy Lord, the living Light flows forth, as in thy Fountain. Nothing of the world can profane or despoil these waters, for they flow from another source.

To reach this purity, this flawless clarity, there must be the love and wonder in thy heart that a child feels when he sees for the first time a flower, or the flight of a bird, or the radiance of a rainbow. All else disappears, save only the wonder and the glory of Truth.

Be as a child. Let all else fall away. Consciousness of the small self, with its history of errors, has no place here. The old image belongs not to the New. Be open only to the New Energies of Love and Truth. Let them fashion a New self, a New Consciousness of wonder and Truth and abide there with me, thy Lord.

***

***

When I said, "I am the Light of the World," it was an absolute, an unchanging Truth, a literal and Divine fact. Without the great ball of fire in the heavens men call the sun, only darkness and death would reign upon this planet. And so it is with the Son of God, for the sun in the heavens is but the focusing of my Light upon all creation on earth, that the Image within each unit, each unique entity, may fructify and awaken and un-fold into its inherent perfection.

I am called by many names. But all know me as the Light of the World.

Be still and know that this Light is both within and without, pressing upon thy soul, thy being. Feel its tender warmth, its fire that does not burn but only caresses and cradles the Divine Word, spoken forth by the Father. For another name for this Light is "Love."

***

Other Worlds

Ring.

"Cynthia, my angel, the snow is coming," says Leonora. "I hate this. Why can't I lift? I am trapped here in this cold. How awful this is!"

"Don't worry," I reply. "You're not trapped. I can get to you in a four-wheel drive vehicle."

"Do you have one of those, Cynthia?"

"No, but I know how to get one. Do you need anything now?"

"No, no, I suppose I am fine," she says reluctantly. "My angel, you will come tomorrow, won't you?"

"I will be there in the morning."

The next morning, in spite of the snow, I make it up Leonora's mountain.

"Good morning," I greet Leonora, half-expecting her to be ill tempered. She hates the cold. "Did you sleep well?" I ask.

"I suppose it was not so... terrible at night, Cynthia. At least they did not show up," she replies.

"They did not show up" does not register at first, so I continue on. "You were able to stay warm enough?"

Yes. I did not leave my bed all night, it was so cold," she "responds. Leonora's cottage is not well insulated, and neither is Leonora, so between the two, the temperature could be 70 degrees and she would still be cold.

Then it registers: "They did not show up?" "Who are they?" I ask.

"That awful woman dressed in period clothing who just walks across my room as if it were hers. And the big, black panther that sometimes sits staring at me from the end of my bed. They are most annoying. I have told them to shoo several times, but they just look at me and ignore anything I have to say. I wish they would stop this. But I suppose they will just continue," she complains.

Now I know what she is talking about. Leonora is tuning into another dimension. "Well, you know, Leonora," I begin, "there are many planes of existence in the same space at the same time. Think of it as a high rise. Let's say you live on the seventh floor and you are looking through the ceiling and seeing the eighth floor. Your mystery guests are in the same space as you, just separated by a floor of consciousness that contains itself to one level."

"Are you saying this is her cottage?" she questions.

"In a manner of speaking, yes," I reply. "Her cottage on a different level that co-exists without being seen. They vibrate differently, which makes them, most of the time, unnoticeable. Like someone who lives in an apartment; they are unnoticeable to their neighbor unless one or the other moves into their space," I proclaim with a sense of authority.

"Well, this is my cottage on this level, and they should not walk across my floor or sit on my bed un-invited on this plane of consciousness. And the next time I see them I am going to tell them so," Leonora says with an air of command in her voice.

***

Truth can never be a patchwork quilt, anymore than sunlight can be both light and shadow.

The shadows in nature reflect only the object the sunlight is shining upon. The shadow belongs not to the light but to the object, the form. Remember this: if there appears to be a shadow upon thine heart, the Light is focusing upon that which is casting the shadow. The shadow is always a sign, a pointer. All that is negative in the human soul casts shadows. And all that is ugly and violent and destructive in the outer world is the work of the Son of Darkness, and it is He who casts these shadows.

These communions shield thee from His mighty efforts to deny, to destroy, and to abolish spiritual Truth.

Be ever awake and aware of His power, for it is rampant at this transition period, where the forces of the Christ are reorienting man's consciousness back to the Eternal Light of God.

Understand this, and be ever attentive to My Voice, which is speaking in thy heart from moment to moment, reminding you, humanity, that you are my spokesman, and the sacred carrier of my Light.

***

***

The Truth begins by being a small beam of Light, even as a single ray of the sun. But this ray of light will intensify until it burns through the old dross, the old selfishness, separating the pure gold from the earthly stuff that has surrounded it.

Give thyself completely to this Light, to Truth, regardless of what pain or suffering the burning process brings forth.

Are you ready for this? Fear not; gold is more beautiful than the dust of the earth that clings to it.

I ask only for thy human self. Thy soul, thy spirit, is already mine, and shines with my Light. The human, the personal self, must also shine with my Light.

Give her to me. This is My Will that must be done. Give her to me; give her wholly to me who am Truth. The Day is at hand. Let it be done.

***

Christmas Fun

Christmas draws near and I know Leonora will spend it alone. On a visit a few days beforehand, I ask her if she would join me, my then-husband, Ralph, and Jan Broan, the woman who introduced us, in celebrating Christmas. She enthusiastically accepts.

"Yes, Cynthia, I would love to go," she says. "Where will we be dining?"

"I thought we would go to the Boar's Head Inn," I reply.

"I will wear my blue suit. I bought it several years back, but it is still lovely." She shows me the suit hanging in the closet. It is blue velvet and looks to be 20 years old.

"I think you will look wonderful in your blue suit, Leonora," I say.

"I am so thin now, Cynthia," Leonora complains. "When I was a young woman I had a smashing figure I weighed 127 pounds and it was all well proportioned. Now my skin just hangs on my bones like clothes hanging on a hanger." She laughs softly as she admires the portrait of herself that is hung over her sofa.

As I leave I tell her, "We will pick you up about 3:00 p.m."

"That will be fine," she replies.

On Christmas Day, 1989, we arrive promptly at Leonora's cottage. She is waiting. Ralph goes to the door to escort her to the car. The walkway is covered with snow and ice. He walks with her ever so carefully, as if caring for china. Jan and I wait in the car.

The Boar's Head is an elegant restaurant and inn just outside Charlottesville and is considered a very special treat. When we arrive the table is not ready yet, and we wait in a room with sofas and a fireplace. The fireplace is blazing, making the room very cozy.

The waiter comes to take our cocktail order. Leonora says to the waiter, "I would love a glass of champagne. I only drink champagne." We all join in and have champagne.

It is heartwarming to watch Leonora and Jan, my two old friends, chatter away like schoolgirls. I have only known these women for a short time four months but both have become my sincere friends. Jan is a young woman in comparison to Leonora a mere 75.

About a half-hour has passed when the maitre'd comes to escort us to our table in the garden room. The room is filled with sunlight from its surrounding windows. A more picturesque view we could not have asked for. The rolling hills and plains are covered by snow. It is perfect.

The menu has just been handed to us when Leonora, looking off at the next table, says, "Look, Cynthia. What a lovely little pickaninny."

I do not know where to hide. I am embarrassed beyond belief. I choose to ignore her and begin chattering.

Leonora assumes I did not hear her and says it again, this time a little louder loud enough for everyone to hear. "LOOK, CYNTHIA, WHAT A LOVELY LITTLE PICKANINNY!"

The room stills with an awkward silence. With apology written from ear to ear, I look over at the child and her parents and say, "Yes Leonora, she is a beautiful little girl."

Mentally and emotionally I had crawled under the table after the first comment. By the time she repeats it, I have dug a hole through the floorboards and tried to disappear. While mentally hiding under the table, I begin to list the possible actions the family might take. I think to myself, Maybe they will ask the waiter to remove us. Or maybe the elegantly dressed father will get up, take his breadbasket, and dump its contents on Leonora's head. Perhaps this is my own desire.

The family of the child says nothing. I am very thankful for the gracious tolerance they and everyone within earshot show my old friend. While this is not the most embarrassing moment in my life, it does rank as one of the top three.

Dinner follows with no further incident.

From the restaurant we all go to my home for more champagne. We are there about an hour when Jan suggests we ride out to her place. I think for certain that Leonora will turn the invitation down. By now she has had many glasses of champagne. But without hesitation, Leonora says, "That is a marvelous idea. YES. Let's do go to Jan's lovely farm!"

Jan lives in Keswick, horse country outside of Charlottes-ville. It is 45 minutes from my house and the opposite direction from Leonora's, but off we go to Jan's to watch the stars and sip more champagne.

While there, Leonora fills her glass several more times. I cannot believe that this 92-year-old woman, weighing all of 90 pounds, has consumed glass after glass of champagne with no seeming effect.

Not once does she say she has had enough or that she is tired and wants to go home. Very much to the contrary; when I suggest she might want to retire for the evening, she immediately rebuts, "I am enjoying myself, Cynthia. Why would I want to go home?"

Leonora out drinks and out lasts all of us that evening. By 10:00 p.m., I am worn out and I tell her we have to take her home. After another 40-minute drive, we deliver her to her door, safe, sound and completely sober.

This is Leonora's last Christmas.

***

The purely human state must inevitably give way that the immortal Self may come into being. This is the purpose of life on earth, and unless this is accomplished, mortality will continue to perpetuate itself in an endless chain of meaningless incarnations.

As we have said, in place of the self thou hast created shines the great Son of God. To understand this statement is to cease creating and re creating a personal self that has no place in Eternity.

The great obstacles to this accomplishment are fear and inertia. Fear of leaving the known, the familiar, for the unknown and unfamiliar; and the inertia that is the manifestation of this fear, stemming from a false sense of security that holds the self down in a self imprisoned state.

If man would only understand that it is he himself who has placed this load upon his back. Therefore, it is he who must shake himself loose from its heavy burden. How can this be done? All through these communications we have answered this question in one form or another.

Think on this question deeply. And then act accordingly, taking no thought, and you will discover a spring of hidden power that will bring to pass miracles undreamed of by the purely human self.

***

***

When you lift into the Light, there can be no lack within thy world, neither here nor there.

Light casts no shadows. The shadows are of the temporal world. Set thy human will and imagination here in the Light, wherein is the fullness of life in all its Divine completeness and perfection. This requires discipline; but how else can you achieve a steadfast purpose, a longed-for goal? There is no other way.

The earth pilgrimage is for this purpose: to rise up out of the earth consciousness, which weighs the self down. As a diver is held underwater by his heavy accoutrements, so the soul is held down by its heavy, earthly vehicles.

To rise up out of this depth, this deep twilight world is man's opportunity now.

Therefore lift, my child, lift into the Eternal Light that is thy Home. Keep thyself one-pointed in thy still center, where the Light shines. The pull is there, drawing thee back up and out of the shadow world.

All that seems to impede thy progress, thy passage, from dark to light, are but aids to push thee upward and forward.

Therefore, tarry not where obstructions seem to be, but push on, never wavering, for the goal is ordained and changes not.

***

Leonora Lifts

Sometime between December 27th and 30th, Leonora is found unconscious by her housekeeper and rushed to Martha Jefferson Hospital. I, along with a few other women she knew including the one who thought I was the devil show up at the hospital. We all gather around, waiting for Leonora to pass. None of us think it will be longer than a few hours. After six or seven hours, we decide to call it a day. Leonora is not ready to go.

For the few remaining days of her life, I sit with Leonora's unconscious body, reading aloud from her journal, talking to her as if we are hanging out at her cottage having one of our usual, unusual conversations. Wiping her face and pushing her wave into place, I often tell her, "You will remember the circle. You can let go and lift now."

On January 2, 1990, when I arrive at Leonora's room, Jan is there. We speak to Leonora and read to her. I tell Leonora that Jan and I will be leaving at 8:00 p.m., and that I will return the next day. At 8:00 we gather our things and leave.

When I get to my car, I realize it is actually ten until eight. I think aloud, "I told Leonora we would leave at 8:00 p.m. But by the time I get back to her room it will be after eight." I decide to go home.

Shortly after arriving home the hospital calls.

Leonora had died at 8:00 p.m. I believe she was waiting for our visit to end before leaving. She needed to "lift" alone.

***

As you feel the Light opening up and cleansing the dark areas of thy consciousness, all is becoming clear and unshadowed. In this tender and gentle Light I dwell, and in the fullness of this quietude, this peace, I speak.

What greater joy can you experience than this, for within this communion, this Oneness, unfolds the Divine purpose of thy life. There is no other purpose than this for thy being. To be a son is to look to the Father with an overflowing love and reverence, for He it is who begot thee, who lovingly brought thee forth to this point of maturity and understanding, that thou mayst return to Him and by His side labor in His vineyards, the vast Universe of His creating. O, my son, I await thee with infinite patience and love. Therefore, falter not, nor loiter upon thy path, lest forgetfulness again overshadow thee, and another will but mine becloud thy memory.

The dawn breaketh, the night is far spent. Keep thy face turned toward the dawn. For in this dawn lies the reality of the New Day on earth.

***

***

Let the Song, which is Life, sing in thy heart this day. Only the Eternal sings, never the temporal, for only echoes can be heard in the temporal world, and never the living Voice.

Hearken, therefore, to the Voice of the Eternal only. It sings the Song of the Joy of Creation and the Love of the Father for His Son. Let no other voice resound throughout thy being this day. Sing, I say, my Song of Life, of Love Eternal, and let its mighty harmony reach to the far corners of the Universe. This is the way of redemption, of the healing of the nations.

To be a part of this vast chorus is to glorify thy God, and to make way for the Kingdom on earth, as in heaven.

***

The Silver Box

David McKnight invited me to the reading of Leonora's will on Wednesday January 10, 1990.

Edie Nash, Leonora's attorney, friend, and landlord, was reading the will, and thoroughly in charge. No relatives came. David, Edie and I were the only people there.

Edie presided over the distribution of Leonora's things. David was to get Leonora's library of books and the picture of Sagatara.

I received the little silver box with the face powder in it. Edie was very hesitant to give the box to me. She said, "This isn't Leonora's handwriting on the will that bequests this to you."

I said, "Of course not. It is my handwriting." The day Leonora called me, convinced she was dying, she asked me to write it in for her. David intervened and persuaded her it was what Leonora wanted.

The art works, antiques, and, I assume, the blue sofa, were all shipped to a relative somewhere.

When I was leaving the cottage, David looked at me and said, "You're upset, aren't you?"

I began to sob. How could I explain how upset I was over this woman's passing or why? After all, I had only known her for four months. But that was the key

I knew her. I knew she didn't like sex. I knew she was afraid of being punished for leaving her father alone when he died. I knew her faith in God. I knew parts of her that possibly no one else knew.

As I wiped my face, David handed me her Murdo Macdonald-Bayne book. "Here," he said. "You should have this." I thanked him and left.

***

When the heart overflows with love for all Beauty and Truth, it is adjusted to the Divine. When these qualities fill the conscious Being, Love pours through which is another name for the Light of God. Know this, and feel its peace, its joy. This is the wonder, the spiritual magic that belongs to the Oneness of Life.

"Be as a little child," He said, for these are the feelings that nourish a child's heart, and unquestioning alignment to the Divine. A child does not question; it accepts and responds naturally, without effort, to the wonder of things.

The great River of Life flows, and sings as it flows, when unobstructed by the underbrush and debris that contaminates its purity.

Let it flow, my child. Let it flow, and it will be a song in thine heart, and all those who hear will lift their voices to its great melody. And so will Harmony be restored on earth, as it was in the beginning; and so will it be again in the Dawn of a New Day.

***

***

Center thy conscious awareness this day on the Son, the great shining Son of God, which is centered or held in place within thee by thy conscious Being, or the I AM which eternally affirms this Truth. This I AM, or affirmation of conscious life, is the Point wherein the infinitude of God's life is focused.

All during this fresh new day that lies before thee, remind thyself constantly of this tremendous fact, that the fullness of God's Presence is centered within thine own self awareness from instant to instant, even as the breath of life flows into thy body and out of thy body from instant to instant.

There can be no moment when this Truth is not operating, is not fully present, whether thou art conscious of it or not. The purpose of thy life is to be conscious of it. Think deeply on this. There can be no instant when God's presence is not fully within reach of thy conscious being, as thy Self, thy immortal Selfhood. Therefore cease thy fostering of this human creature, but see only thy God-Self as the One reality of thy existence, not to be realized in some future heaven, but to be known here and now, in this place, at this time. Even so will thy God-Self come forth and become thy self, closing the gap between the human and the Divine.

***

Leonora and I Become One

Leonora always has the last word. This was even true at the service that was held on her behalf.

After Leonora's passing, David McKnight arranged, as requested by Leonora, to have her ashes dispersed over a beautiful mountain in the Blue Ridge. I was surprised when David picked Afton Mountain instead of Leonora's Monticello, but I thought maybe Leonora needed a new view.

On March 4th 1990, we all met at the Holiday Inn Afton Mountain, where we gathered around a table to speak about our particular relationship with Leonora. There were seven or eight of us: Jan, David and his wife, Mary, Ralph, my daughter Corie, one or two others, and I. But not the lady who thought I was the devil.

David McKnight started the eulogy with his remembrances of Leonora as part of America's spiritual aristocracy, "a class act," and "true royalty." Everyone concurred. I believe the exact statement was, "She was as close to royalty as this country gets."

As it came my turn to speak, David looked at me and said, "Cynthia, you knew Leonora better than anyone here." Everyone at the table looked in my direction. I began to shift in my seat as I responded. I did not want to tarnish the crown they had placed on her royal head. But I said what I felt in my heart. "I certainly knew Leonora differently than you all. Leonora was a difficult woman. Trying, impatient and amazing. I will always remember her. She was, is, and will be my friend, and I will miss her."

With that we went down the mountain to an overlook where we all toasted with champagne our friend who had such a rich, full and long life. As we each stood holding Leonora's ashes in one hand, and a paper cup of champagne in the other, people began to throw her remains. Leonora would have loved the scene, although she would have insisted on crystal goblets for the champagne.

As I stood there crying, my nose leaking, and mouth wide open, I closed my eyes and said my final goodbye. I threw her ashes. At that moment, a gust of wind arose and blew Leonora right back into my face. I ingested her through my mouth, nose, and eyes.

Wiping my face, I joked, "Leonora and I truly have become one."

***

Absorb into thy heart the resurrecting energies all about thee. These living energies are pouring into the earth to awaken all that sleeps within the natural world. Absorb into thy being this ecstasy, this life force, this creative fire. It will consume that which encloses the self, and liberate the New growth that lies dormant there. Let this life force flood thy being, thy world. It will strengthen and illumine.

Nothing stands still. All is alive and in perpetual movement, in creative joy. Fear not. The heartbeat is life Eternal. All is unfolding in the Eternal. Live each moment as a gift of the Eternal. Listen to the word that is ever sounding within thy Being. The word is the Christ, is Creation, is life Eternal.

***

***

This is the season to lift up, to raise the consciousness the Light of the Christ, the risen Christ.

It is a crucial moment, where the fullness of Light should flood through the human heart and soul. "Partake of my body, and drink of my blood," He said. To do this is to walk His path of Love and Light. Each traveler on the way is watched over by Him. You have but to stretch forth thy hand to touch His garment, for He is very near. To remember this is to safeguard thyself from all the errors the flesh is heir to, for one cannot look in two directions at once. The choice is ever before man.

To be the "Image and Likeness" of God is to be as a polished mirror, that He may see Himself reflected there. How else can man be the "Image and Likeness," save only to reflect Him as He is.

***

The Journal's Journey

In February of 1991, I decided to pack a few of my treasures and set forth on developing my career as a psychic. I moved back to the area that seemed to hold the most support for this bold venture: Virginia. One of the things that made the journey with me was Leonora's journal. I was living in a small apartment and was seldom there. So I kept the precious journal where I thought it would be safest in my office.

I placed the journal and a few other items in a file box, labeled it, and stored it in the office storage room. The only way into the storage space was through the lobby, and although it had a copier and postage machine in it that were used daily, it remained locked when my office mates or I weren't there. Convinced it was totally safe, I never gave it another thought.

In March of 1993, our lease was up and we all moved to different locations. When I went to pack, the file box containing the journal was gone. No one had seen it. It was as if it had disappeared. I was so disappointed in myself. I searched until there was nowhere left to search. Literally, the office was empty. After a good deal of kicking myself in the ass, I finally let it go and made peace with Leonora and myself.

Ten years later, after several moves from coast to coast, a divorce, and a new husband, I was back in Virginia living down the street from a client I met while in Charlottesville. Robert, now my friend, was having garage dysfunction, and I offered to help him bring order to his chaos. We worked in his garage for a week, unpacking, organizing, and sorting. We found things Robert had had in storage for decades.

As we got to the very last boxes, there it was a copy of the journal! When I originally put the journal back together, I had made a copy for Robert to give to his brother in-law for revision. This was the complete journal, both handwritten as well as typed. Nothing was missing. Robert had moved shortly after I gave the journal to him, had packed it in a box and had forgotten all about it.

I felt as if Leonora had been returned to me. I brought the journal home, and set it on a shelf. I thought to myself, "Isn't it wonderful to find it again?"

It wasn't too long before a message came loud and clear. "I didn't go through all this trouble to bring my journal back to you, Cynthia, for it to sit on your shelf. You have work to do."

I answered aloud as if Leonora was next to me supervising a serving of milk toast. "OK, Leonora."

I knew it wasn't just the journal that had made the journey, but Leonora herself. The circle of our souls that Leonora and I had made the day she thought she was dying had not been broken. Apparently, all our vowing and declaring worked.

Leonora has come to help me with my work. Her promise to me, as mine to her, is being kept.

***

As the New Day dawns, all that is hidden will be revealed. The Light of the Christ will flood out of the dark corners the secret sins, the ancient wrongs, the undergrowth of vice and corruption. It is the time of retribution, of revelation. No soul will be untouched, for the Light will pierce the darkness everywhere and lay bare that which is concealed therein.

To be aware of this is to open all the windows and doors of the self, and let in the Light, that all that lurks in the shadows may be flushed out.

It is a time of renewal, of resurrection, of rebirth. As man understands this, as his soul lifts to the Christos, he will remember who he is, and once again will know his way back to the Father's House as it was shown him some 2,000 years ago when the Great Cosmic Drama of Light and Dark was played out on the earth stage for all to see and profit by.

Once again the stage is set and the Mighty Conflict will unfold. O, be thou ready and prepared, for the hour draws near and is at hand.

***

***

Many problems will arise, my child. Difficult challenges will come at this time, but they come only to be met by the Truth that has been given thee in these communications.

The Path lies not through sunlight all the way, but also through the shadows shadows which are cast by the image, not of Truth or God, but of the old, the World self.

This is the great contest; the conflict between these two images, which is life on earth today, and few embodied souls will escape this conflict.

To understand this is to be prepared, and thereby is victory assured.

To let thyself be confused or fearful at these moments is to give over to the World-self and to forsake the One speaking in thy heart.

There are times when the bodily self or World-self will seem to usurp the power of God, and speak and act in defiance of the One Law.

But be not afraid. These states are as nothing, and are powerless in the Light of this law.

As we have said, all that lurks within the darkness must be flushed out into the Light.

Rejoice that this is taking place, both within and without, and watch thy fears as they dissolve into their primal nothingness as the Light of Truth is focused upon them.

Be at peace and remember: the Father loveth the Son, and His everlasting arms are around Him.

The Cottage Today

The Roosevelt-Nichols cottage is now a part of the Jefferson Institute for International Studies. For anyone with a desire for a look, the May 1941 issue of Life magazine has a several-page spread on the cottage as it was then. The magazine layout looks almost identical to the cottage I visited, with the exception of Leonora's personal art, antiques and, of course her blue sofa.

***

You are beginning to absorb into your whole being the deep meaning of these communications.

The Light of Truth, as it flows from the Higher Self, is now radiating through thine entire being. To limit thyself in any way or direction is to deny this radiation. The discipline needed is to hold and sustain it.

To realize that there is nothing in all creation but God and His Son is to be free of all that denies or departs from the One Truth. How then can you fear or doubt. The world as it appears to be is this denial. But look not upon the world, for God's Son is not of the world but of the Kingdom where God and He are One, where God and you are One. To accept this absolute is to reflect the Father as His Image and Likeness. This is Man.

Keep thyself pointed in this One way, at One with the Father and His only-begotten Son. This realization, even though it comes as a brief flash, is the link in the great chain of Light that will release men from their self-created dungeons of darkness and despair. To be this link of Light is God's will for you. As each self or soul turns toward this Light so will he, too, be an Eternal link in a Universe of Light.

To radiate this Truth is thy mission.

I have spoken. Rejoice, and be at peace.

***

The Cottage Today

The Conversations Resume

I am driving home in the rain, wavering as to whether to be diligent and write more reminiscences about Leonora, or take the afternoon off for a pedicure. A familiar voice goes off in my head.

"Cynthia, my angel, write three more lovely little stories about me. Then go and get your toes painted."

"OK," I say aloud, as if she was sitting next to me. "But only three. I want a pedicure."

"Well, let's tell them," the voice continues.

"Wait a minute I'm not home yet."

"Of course, my angel. Do be careful in the rain. But hurry. I am waiting for you, my angel."

On another occasion, I am thinking about what reminiscences of Leonora to relate next when I hear, "Cynthia, my angel, never have doubts about your ability to write, for I have chosen you to write my story."

"Thank you, Leonora," I think. "I promise I will always remember your faith in my ability to write. And you know I keep my promises."

***

As we have said, the human being is a vital part of the living universe, and in reality man's body is composed of the same substance and energy that flows into all the diverse forms within the natural world that surrounds him, whether it be a tree, or a stone, or a star.

What is this energy but the perpetual movement of particles of light in various degrees of frequencies and vibrations?

To see the body as a composition of minute atoms and molecules of light moving in perfect harmony with the Universal Light of creation will eliminate from the subconscious the false picture of a body of dense matter, of physical flesh and bones, susceptible to disease, disaster and death.

This understanding will bring in the New era of healing, with the realization that disease is impossibility, as is any derangement of the energy patterns created by God. As man reaches out to this Archetypal world with his Intuitive mind, so will he know himself as God has created him, and so will he experience the fundamental, simple and perfect unity between all creatures and all beings upon this planet. He will discover that through this oneness flows the great Law that binds all together in a partnership of love and collaboration

***

***

These recordings, or Transmissions, can be released to the world as a "testament of Light." This is, indeed, the moment on earth that can be called the Transition period. For, as the Divine solar energies pour in little by little, the transformation from dark to light will take place.

To give thyself to these energies of Light is thy deep desire. So be it. As you listen and record, the Light will use that which you are offering, a mind-heart lifted to its level. Rejoice that this is taking place.

There are countless seeds in the human kingdom, consciousness out in the wider world, waiting for the Light, longing for the Light. And therefore there will be, eventually, a general awakening to the Light.

These communications will be one of the many Solar rays that are gathering on earth, that these seeds or potentials may fructify and rise up. God and His Son are the One and only Source of Light. As man evolves and becomes more and more conscious of his True Self as God's Son, he becomes a part of this One Light.

Meditate upon this, and be at Peace.

***

Two Dragons

While writing of my adventure with Leonora, my husband Jon and I took great care to have the information about her father and childhood in the Lawrenceville Artist Community correct in name and description, including doing research at George Mason University on biographies of her distinguished family members and on the community she grew up in. Little did we know this would initiate another adventure with Leonora.

After several weeks of all-day and all-night writing and editing, we decided to take a well deserved break and visit friends in Williamsburg, New York. We had a great dinner and morning visit with Cosimo and Sarah. As we were leaving their home, we asked if they knew where Bronxville was. We knew only that it was near New York City. It turns out we were 30 minutes away. We said our goodbyes and set out for Bronxville.

At this time, the only thing we knew about the area was that it was called Lawrence Park, or Lawrenceville, and that it existed somewhere within the Village of Bronxville. When we exited the parkway, the first thing we saw was an older lady walking across the street. We pulled over and asked her for directions to Bronxville. She pointed, "You are already here."

We drove through the village hoping to find a sign indicating Lawrenceville. We stopped at the Lawrence Hospital in hopes that someone would know. Two gentlemen we met there both had grown up in the area, and neither knew of Lawrenceville or Lawrence Park.

We knew by the name of the hospital that we should not give up. My husband walked into the local pharmacy and asked a policeman and a customer if either had heard of the community. The customer said, "Yes, Lawrenceville is right down the street. Turn at the real estate office and after the tennis courts." Thus we found the entrance to Lawrenceville.

The street was literally a yellow brick road. We followed the road up narrow winding streets filled with beautiful old homes. The architecture and layout was unique, like none other we had seen. There were plaques on the houses stating which artist the house was built for. We parked the car and began walking up to people's houses, reading the plaques and generally looking around.

Jon struck up a conversation with a resident of the area who was outside gardening. He asked her if she knew where the Nichols house was. She said no; but she had a book listing all the houses in the community and the artists they had belonged to. She kindly went inside her home and came back with the book. We sat on her porch and looked through the book, taking notes. Under Henry Hobart Nichols' name we found the address. We asked where it was, and she said, "Oh, that's West Lawrence Park. The homes are bigger over there. Just go back over the parkway and take a left." We thanked her for her help and bolted back to the car. Not more than 20 minutes and a few wrong turns later we found ourselves sitting in front of Leonora Nichols' family home where she had grown up and lived until her father died in 1962.

I could feel butterflies in my stomach as we rang the doorbell. Not really knowing how to explain what we where doing there, I fumbled out something like, "I knew a lady who lived here. May I see your garden?"

The lady of the house looked a little bewildered, but my husband and I apparently looked harmless enough. She walked us around back. "Now the garden is not in bloom," she said, "so you will not see it at its best."

Her husband was sitting with a confused look on his face as he watched two strangers his wife had just invited into their garden. Too immersed in looking over the yard, I barely introduced myself. There it was the back yard where Leonora's father painted her portrait. The slate bench under the tree was still there. I excitedly told Jon that I recognized everything.

I calmed down a bit and was able to explain to the lady and her husband how I came to know Leonora, and what sparked our pilgrimage. Her husband began to relax and became interested in this bit of history of his house, and the tale from his community.

The lady became a fountain of information about the house. "The last owner almost destroyed the fireplace mantle. They had to call in an art specialist to repair it. It is a very rare piece," she said. "Would you like to see it?"

"Of course," I replied. We were hoping all the time she would invite us in.

I walked in after Jon, entering rather shyly. Jon immediately started exploring the main room, rousing their teenager from the couch with his presence. After a few moments, I followed him into what was Henry Hobart Nichol's studio, now a den. Jon was standing silently in front of the fireplace staring at it. I turned through the entrance and there it was a magnificent mantle of carved wood. It took me a minute for the design to emerge. As it did, I began to shake in my shoes.

Jon said, "Look honey, two dragons. Can you believe this?"

I looked at the women and said, "I can't believe this is real. It's two dragons." She looked oddly at me. I continued, "Two dragons. That is the name of our company. We're both dragons." I took out a business card from my purse and showed it to her. We all sat there stunned.

The lady of the house became enthralled with the coincidence. She began showing us the carved figureheads around the dining room. Jon busily snapped pictures of the fireplace as I walked into the kitchen where, off to the right, was a sunroom. You could almost see Leonora sitting there. The truly odd thing was the woman had it decorated in blue. Over the mantle in the dining room she had an angel. I almost cried. I told her about Leonora calling me her angel.

In the stairwell a large, stained glass window with a blue design, similar to the one on my silver box, cast Leonora's energy everywhere. We looked at the two-dragon fireplace mantle once again before leaving and left half in shock, half in joy.

That day we knew there is a bigger connection to every person we meet bigger than we can ever fathom.

***

Revelation wipes out time with all its accumulated ills, and brings into focus the Eternal, the Divine.

Thou art standing at this timeless moment in the Eternal Light; and what is that Light but the radiance of Love itself? To feel this ecstatic Truth is to be it, to partake of it.

The Divine message of the Fountain of Light was Love revealing Itself, symbolically, for thine understanding.

To awaken thee to the full impact of this revealed Truth has been the primary purpose of these communications, for the Source that projected that image into thy soul is the same Source from which these communions are flowing.

To experience Truth is to know it forever. We have led you to this moment of illumination that thou mayst equate and relate all that is to come to this Supreme fact upon which eternal life rests: that the Source of thy life, of all life, is Love Itself. This one Truth fulfills the One Law. When this is deeply understood and experienced as revelation, all else disappears.

***

***

All who read these pages will find only one message running through them, even as a shining thread of gold, of light; and each communication brings a variation on that one theme. And what is that theme but the Eternal Truth that I AM here, within I, the living God.

And thou who read these words, thou who art man, man of my creating, art the beloved Son, even as the Christ revealed. The denial of this Truth is the darkness spreading over the face of the earth.

I speak now to those who have ears to hear, who offer their hearts in love and service, and thereby have the capacity to listen to my voice, speaking in the stillness of their deeper selfhood. And I say the hour has come for the fulfilling of the Law, both in the destruction of those forces that deny and defame it, and in the liberation of those energies that affirm and fulfill it. Even so must it be, for there is sowing and reaping, and this is the working out of the Law that changeth not.

Oh, thou who art listening, who art the sons and daughters of God, be not dismayed, for so will a new Peace spread out over the world, and upon this Peace rests the Tabernacle of the New Jerusalem, or the New Day on earth.

Amen.

***

***

Let thy Fountain of Light flow freely now. The waters are the waters of renewal, of revitalization. This ecstatic freedom will irradiate thy Spirit, thy self.

Understand what we are saying: the symbol shown you in vision was projected by thy soul as a guide for you to follow. This thy path. Transparent Light holds no flaws, no darkness. Keep thine inward gaze upon It.

There is no need for further instruction at this time. Be still, and absorb and embody all that has been given thee.

Live it.

Live it now.

***

The Promise